بسم الله الرحمن الرحيم

ONE HUNDRED AND FIFTY LIFE LESSONS

By Grand Ayatullah Makārim Shīrāzī

TABLE OF CONTENTS

An Introduction to the Text

After the Holy Quran, our greatest resource is the Sunnah of the Prophet (ṣ) and the invaluable traditions of the Ahl al-Bayt (ʿa). In essence, these two are what comprise the 'two weighty things' which the Prophet (ṣ) left for us after his death. He stated that if we were to take hold of these two things and abide by them, we would be protected from deviation and misguidance. Unfortunately, even though these traditions are an ocean of knowledge and understanding, they have remained thus far unknown and unrecognized. If we were to tap into these traditions, we would really be tapping into the very knowledge of life itself and it would help us resolve many of the problems that we see within ourselves and within the society.

This book which you are now reading is a selection of various traditions, along with a short explanation in regards to them. These one hundred and fifty selections are taken from lectures that were given at the Imam Ḥusayn (ʿa) Mosque in Tehran, Iran. Each week, one tradition was selected and lectured on, and the participants memorized them and attempted to implement them during that one week period.

The demand for these lessons was so high that we decided to print them in a small book-type format. In this way, an individual can easily increase their understanding of Islam through the study of this short work. What is more important than reading and understanding though, is the implementation of these lessons into one's life. Let us all come forward and seek from God the ability and blessings of properly understanding these traditions and then implementing and applying them within ourselves, as well as others.

The Blessed City of Qum, Iran
Nāṣir Makārim Shīrāzī
The Month of Shawwāl, 1397

LESSON ONE

THOUGHT, CONTEMPLATION, AND REFLECTION

Tradition:

أَلَا لَا خَيْرَ فِى عِلمٍ لَيْسَ فِيهِ تَفَهُّمٌ

Know that there is no benefit in knowledge without thought!

أَلَا لَا خَيْرَ فِى قَرَائَةٍ لَيْسَ فِيها تَدَبُّرٌ

Know that there is no benefit in the recitation of the Quran if there is no contemplation!

أَلَا لَا خَيْرَ فِى عِبادَةٍ لَيْسَ فِيها تَفَكُّرٌ

Know that worship without reflection is without effect![1]

Brief Commentary:

Filling the mind with all sorts of scientific formulas, logical precepts, philosophical principles, and all other types of knowledge is of extremely little value unless it is accompanied with proper thinking and a clear and accurate worldview. If one is not familiar with the principles of life, then all of these things drop dramatically in value. Similarly, the effects of reading the Holy Quran become almost insignificant if it is not accompanied with contemplation and attention into the depths of meaning found within it. Similarly, worship without reflection and the use of the intellect is like a body without a spirit and it lacks the loftier effects that such worship can have.

---

[1] Uṣūl al-Kāfī, vol. 1, p. 36. This tradition can also be found in Tuḥaf al-ʿUqūl

Lesson Two
The Measure of Reflection

Tradition:

صَلَاحُ حَالِ التَّعَايُشِ وَالتَّعَاشُرِ مِلْءُ مِكْيَالٍ ثُلُثَاهُ فِطْنَةٌ وَثُلُثُهُ تَغَافُلٌ

Imam Ṣādiq (ʿa) is narrated to have said: The reformation of life is completed through a measure that is two thirds caution and one third a lack of care and attention![1]

Brief Commentary:

Nothing can ever be completed without careful study, planning, and cautiousness; at the same time, nothing can ever be completed without a lack of care as well. Now the question is how can such a thing be, since it appears to be a total contradiction in terms? The answer is that if we wanted to do something without study, proper planning, and attention, then we would be unable to take that to completion. Yet, if we wanted to plan for all the possible things that could take place or could go wrong, then we would become bogged down with all the possibilities, and even simple tasks would end up taking years upon years of difficult planning and thought. In a nutshell, over thinking and over planning play a role similar to a lack of thought and a lack of proper planning. This is the explanation behind the tradition where it mentions that planning and attention to detail comprise two thirds of this issue, while one third is comprised of a lack of attention to detail.

[1] Tuḥaf al-ʿUqūl, p. 267.

Lesson Three

They Pay So Much Attention to the Food That They Eat, But...

Tradition:

عَجِبْتُ لِمَنْ يَتَفَكَّرُ فِي مَأْكُولِهِ كَيْفَ لَا يَتَفَكَّرُ فِي مَعْقُولِهِ، فَيُجَنِّبُ بَطْنَهُ مَا يُؤْذِيهِ وَيُودِعُ صَدْرَهُ مَا يُرْدِيهِ

Imam Ḥasan (ʿa) is narrated to have said: I am surprised at those who reflect on the food that they are going to eat and yet they do not think at all in regards to the food of their soul. They stay away from unhealthy food, but they fill their hearts with various destructive matters.[1]

Brief Commentary:

Just as the Imam (ʿa) has mentioned, people are very careful in regards to what they eat. They will only eat foods which they trust and if there is a ten percent chance of illness or food poisoning, they will not even think of eating that food. Some people go beyond this and follow all sorts of nutritional precepts and rules which they believe will aid them in regards to their health. In a nutshell, people care deeply about the food that they eat.

Yet when it comes to the food pertaining to their soul, they take in whatever they find, irregardless of how it will affect them. Even if they are about to ingest something which has a 95% chance of illness and the potential to poison their soul, they don't really pay any attention and they carelessly take it in. If people tell them words of slander and backbiting, they sit and listen without any fear. This is in reality the equivalent of someone placing a plate of spoiled food in front of them, which will certainly make them ill, and their eating of it.

What we must realize is that various things which relate to the spirit naturally have an effect on the spirit, and the spirit

[1] Safīnat al-Biḥār, Section on Food.

grows or diminishes as a result of what it takes in. This is exactly like when we eat food and our bodies either grow strong from it, or grow weak and become ill as a result of it. It is truly amazing that people pay such detailed attention to the foods related to their physical bodies, but are so utterly careless when it comes to the food of their souls.

Lesson Four
The Role of the Pen

Tradition:

لَمْ أَرَ باكِيًا أَحْسَنَ تَبَسُّمًا مِنَ القَلَمِ!

Imam Ṣādiq (ʻa) has said: I have not seen anything weeping as beautifully as a pen when it smiles.[1]

Brief Commentary:

The pen is an amazing means of the expression of various human emotions and points of wisdom. It can be said that the pen is what gave rise to the concept of civilization and it is what allows society to function in such a smooth fashion. The pen expresses the pain that the people feel and it also expresses the vitality and life that is within them. It is the medium that expresses love, excitement, sorrow, and the very beauty of life.

At the same time, if this pen falls into the hands of unworthy individuals, it weeps blood rather than ink, and its smile transforms into a cruel smirk which helps unseat the highest of human values and morals.

[1] From the book: Laṭā'if wa Ẓarā'if.

Lesson Five
In Between Two Great Responsibilities

Tradition:

الْمُؤْمِنُ بَيْنَ مَخَافَتَيْنِ: ذَنْبٌ قَدْ مَضَى لَا يَدْرِي مَا صَنَعَ اللهُ فِيهِ، وَعُمُرٌ قَدْ بَقِيَ لَا يَدرِي مَا يَكْتَسِبُ فِيهِ مِنَ الْمَهَالِكِ

Imam Ṣādiq (ʻa) has stated: A faithful person is always worried about two things. The first includes the past sins for which he does not know how God will act in regards to them, while the second is for what is left of his life, during which he is uncertain of how he will behave.[1]

Brief Commentary:

The clearest sign of faith is a sense of responsibility towards one's actions, as well as the duties that one must abide by. Someone who senses these two responsibilities will always be thinking of ways to fulfill them as well as making up for past lapses. Such a person will always have this thought in mind of how they can best act in light of their duties and how they can make use of the time that they have left.

[1] Uṣūl al-Kāfī, vol. 2, p. 7.

Lesson Six
Factors that Lead Towards Societal Destruction

Tradition:

أرْبَعٌ لَا يَدْخُلُ بَيْتًا وَاحِدَةٌ مِنْهَا إلَّا خَرِبَ وَلَم يَعْمُرْ بِالْبَرَكَةِ: الْخِيَانَةُ وَالسَّرِقَةُ، وَشُرْبُ الْخَمْرِ، وَالزِّنَا

There are four things, which, even if one of them is present in a home, will lead to its destruction and God's blessings will not bring it to flourishment. These are treachery, thievery, the consumption of alcohol, and acts against chastity.[1]

Brief Commentary:

This is something which not only applies to a home, but it also applies to a society as well. For example, when treachery becomes commonplace and permeates society, then the spirit of trust leaves it. When thievery becomes commonplace in society, then that society will be robbed of peace and security. When the use of alcohol becomes commonplace, people will not think properly, children will be born with various problems, and the youth will not utilize their time and energy in the proper manner. When the society becomes affected by a lack of chastity, then the foundation of the family will be shaken and future generations will be pulled towards corruption.

[1] From Nahj al-Faṣāḥah.

Lesson Seven

Laziness and Poverty

Tradition:

إِنَّ الْأَشْيَاءَ لَمَّا ازْدَوَجَتْ، ازْدَوَجَ الْكَسَلُ وَالْعَجْزُ فَنَتَجَ مِنْهُمَا الفَقْرُ

Imam ʻAlī (ʻa) is narrated to have said: On the day that all things were paired, laziness and weakness were joined with one another and they gave birth to poverty.[1]

Brief Commentary:

Everything is gained through hard work and struggle, and this is a reality that Islam has taught us. Laziness, a lack of desire, and escape from the hardships and difficulties that one faces in life is something that is not in concordance with faith. These are things that will bring about poverty and not just financial poverty, but poverty in one's morals and spiritual state as well. People of faith should try their utmost to be independent from all perspectives and not rely on others for assistance.

[1] Biḥār al-Anwār, vol. 78, p. 59; Tuḥaf al-ʻUqūl, p. 158.

Lesson Eight

The Descent of Knowledge upon the Hearts

Tradition:

يَا بُنَيَّ، إِنَّ اللهَ - عَزَّ وَجَلَّ - يُحيي القُلُوبَ بِنُورِ الحِكْمَةِ كَما يُحْيِى الْأَرْضَ بِوَابِلِ السَّمَاءِ

Luqmān, the famous sage, is reported to have said: Oh my son, God enlivens the hearts of the people through the light of knowledge and understanding, just like the dead earth is brought to life with the rains that descend from the skies.[1]

Brief Commentary:

The heart is much like a fertile orchard which has various trees and plants growing within it. It possesses different herbs, fruit bearing trees, and flowers. If these plants are watered and taken care of in the proper way, then all of the plants will reach their full potential and beauty. The means through which this orchard is watered is through the rain of knowledge and understanding. It's for this same reason that the hearts of those without knowledge are completely barren and dead, unable to give fruit or anything else of value. In all situations, we must strive to enliven ourselves with the light of knowledge and understanding.

[1] From the book Biḥār al-Anwār, vol. 1.

Lesson Nine
The Root of Arrogance

Tradition:

مَا مِنْ رَجُلٍ تَكَبَّرَ أَوْ تَجَبَّرَ إِلَّا لِذِلَّةٍ وَجَدَهَا فِي نَفْسِهِ

Imam Ṣādiq (ʻa) is narrated to have said: There is no person who acts arrogantly towards others except for a weakness which he senses within himself.[1]

Brief Commentary:

Today, it has been shown through psychological studies that the root of arrogance and prideful behavior can be found in a feeling of inferiority that people possess within themselves. People who suffer from this inferiority complex attempt to use this misguided technique to show themselves as being superior to others. Yet, this type of behavior only adds to their inferiority because people recognize them for who they are, and over time, this increases the people's hate and disgust for them. This psychological issue has been mentioned over a thousand years ago by Imam Ṣādiq (ʻa). On the other hand, people who have faith are affected by a particular inner state which inclines them towards modesty and humbleness.

---

[1] Biḥār al-Anwār, vol. 73, p. 225.

Lesson Ten
Three Valuable Things In the View of God

Tradition:

ثَلَاثٌ تَخْرُقُ الْحُجُبَ وَتَنْتَهِي إِلَى مَا بَيْنَ يَدَيِ اللهِ:

صَرِيرُ أَقْلَامِ الْعُلَمَاءِ

وَوَطْيُ أَقْدَامِ الْمُجَاهِدِينَ

وَصَوْتُ مَغَازِلِ الْمُحْصَنَاتِ

The Prophet (ṣ) is narrated to have said: There are three things which tear the veils and reach God Almighty's presence: The sound of the scholar's pen as he begins to write, the sound of the footsteps of the warriors (Mujāhids) on the battlefield, and the sound of the weaving machine of the chaste women.

Brief Commentary:

There are three sounds which extend to the very source of creation and continue on for eternity. The first of these sounds is that of the pen, even though it simply whispers through the night and has virtually no sound. The second is the sound of the warrior's footsteps as he maneuvers towards the enemy in defending himself, and the third is the sound of hard work and struggle, even if it may seem to be very simple at first glance. A sound society is composed of these three important facets: knowledge, struggle against one's enemies, and hard work and effort.

Lesson Eleven
The Martyrdom of Imam Ḥusayn ('a)

Tradition:

إِنَّ لِقَتْلِ الْحُسَيْنِ حَرَارَةً فِي قُلُوبِ الْمُؤْمِنِينَ لَنْ تَبْرَدَ أَبَدًا

The Prophet (ṣ) is narrated to have said: The martyrdom of Imam Ḥusayn ('a) has created a fire and heat in the hearts of the faithful which can never be extinguished.[1]

Brief Commentary:

There have been many different wars throughout history and almost without exception, they have been all but forgotten just a few months or years after they ended. Yet, if someone fights in the way of God and struggles in the path of liberating his fellow human beings, then this is something that can never be forgotten. This is because fighting for the sake of God, as well as concepts like freedom, honor, and dignity are things which never get old, nor are they ever forgotten. Imam Ḥusayn ('a) and his companions fought for these very concepts and it is for this reason that they will never be forgotten.

---

[1] Mustadrak al-Wasā'il, vol. 2, p. 217.

Lesson Twelve

Two Signs of a True Muslim

Translation:

لَا تَنظُرُوا إِلَى كَثْرَةِ صَلَاتِهِمْ وَصَوْمِهِمْ وَكَثْرَةِ الْحَجِّ وَالْمَعْرُوفِ وَطَنْطَنَتِهِمْ بِاللَّيْلِ، وَلَكِنِ انْظُرُوا إِلَى صِدْقِ الْحَدِيثِ وَأَدَاءِ الْأَمَانَةِ

The Prophet (ṣ) is narrated to have said: Do not look only at the number of prayers, fasting sessions, Ḥajj pilgrimages, night vigils, or good acts (towards others) of the people (even though these things are important). Rather, look at their truthfulness and trustworthiness.[1]

Brief Commentary:

When one looks at the Islamic traditions, it becomes clear that there are two definite signs of a true Muslim: truthfulness and trustworthiness. Even though acts of worship like prayer, fasting, and the Ḥajj pilgrimage are all very important and instrumental in the growth of human beings, still these cannot be considered the only signs of faith and Islam in an individual. They must be accompanied with truthfulness and trustworthiness.

[1] Taken from the book Safīnat al-Biḥār.

Lesson Thirteen
The Fire of Wrath!

Tradition:

إِنَّ هٰذَا الْغَضَبَ جَمْرَةٌ مِنَ الشَّيْطَانِ تُوقَدُ فِي قَلْبِ ابْنِ آدَمَ

Imam Bāqir (ʿa) is narrated to have said: Anger and wrath are burning flames from Satan which are lit in the innermost sections of the heart of man.[1]

Brief Commentary:

It is extremely rare for someone to do something or make a decision while in a state of rage and not be regretful of what has taken place later on. This is because rage and anger cause the intellect and the process of correct decision making to completely fall by the wayside. The nervous system also becomes agitated in a way where the individual may do something that they will regret for the rest of their lives. When a person becomes angry, they must quickly contain their anger and work to extinguish it as soon as possible. If they don't do this, the fire of this rage may consume both themselves, as well as those who are around them!

[1] Biḥār al-Anwār, vol. 73, p. 278.

Lesson Fourteen
The Sources of Wealth

Tradition:

اطْلُبُواْ الرِّزْقَ فِي خَبَايَا الْأَرْضِ

The Prophet (ṣ) is narrated to have said: Seek your sustenance in the hiding places of this earth.[1]

Brief Commentary:

During a time when mining for minerals was not really understood that well, the Prophet (ṣ) instructed the Muslims that if they wish to seek their sustenance, they should look within the depths of the earth. Such instructions show both the wisdom of the Islamic teachings, as well as the importance of struggle in the way of gaining a lawful and honorable sustenance.

[1] Narrated from the book Nahj al-Faṣāḥah.

Lesson Fifteen
The Worst of Professions

Tradition:

شَرُّ الْمَكَاسِبِ كَسْبُ الرِّبَا

The Prophet (ṣ) is narrated to have said: The worst earnings are the earnings mixed with usury (Ribā).

إِذَا أَرَادَ اللهُ بِقَوْمٍ هَلَاكًا ظَهَرَ فِيهِمُ الرِّبَا

Imam Ṣādiq (ʻa) is narrated to have said: Whenever God wishes to destroy a nation, usury becomes evident amongst them.[1]

Brief Commentary:

In spite of the widespread prevalence of usury in our world today and the seemingly addictive dependence of the world economy upon it, there is no question that usury as a system ends up destroying the society in which it is allowed to exist. Usury causes wealth to accumulate in an unnatural way in the hands of a few individuals and this unjust division is the root of various societal and ethical ills.

---

[1] Taken from the book Wasa'īl al-Shīʻah, vol. 12, pgs. 426 and 427.

Lesson Sixteen
Rulership and Slavery

Tradition:

امْنُنْ عَلَى مَنْ شِئْتَ تَكُنْ أَمِيرَهُ
وَاحْتَجْ إِلَى مَنْ شِئْتَ تَكُنْ أَسِيرَهُ
وَاسْتَغْنِ عَمَّنْ شِئْتَ تَكُنْ نَظِيرَهُ

Imam ʿAlī (ʿa) is narrated to have said: Do good towards whomever you like and you will rule over them! Be self sufficient over whomever you like and you will become equal to them! And be dependent on whomever you like and you will become their slave.

Brief Commentary:

When it comes to the social interactions of people, this is a rule which holds completely true in regards to their relationships with one another. Those who consistently give are always at an advantage, while those who consistently receive are always at a disadvantage. This also applies to nations as well, for if a nation is one that primarily receives from others, then it is treated much as an inferior and slave. Those nations that give are treated as the superiors of these other nations. A true Muslim is one who establishes a social relationship with others based on both giving and receiving, and not simply based on one of these aspects. Those who receive aid should be those who are disabled and truly unable to work or provide for themselves.

Lesson Seventeen

Religious Falsity and Posturing

Tradition:

لَا تُرَاءِ بِعَمَلِكَ مَنْ لَا يُحْيِي وَلَا يُمِيتُ وَلَا يُغْنِي عَنْكَ شَيْئًا

Imam Ṣādiq (ʻa) is narrated to have said: Do not perform good actions for the sake of posturing and showing off to people who neither have the power of life or death, nor do they have the power of solving any problems for you![1]

Brief Commentary:

Those who become used to showing off and posturing in front of others end up living lives that are completely empty and devoid of any substance. Due to this manner of living, their lives begin to lack all felicity and happiness. They only possess the very outer aspects of religion and religiosity, and they suffice with dry rituals when it comes to their religious practices. It is for this same reason that Islam has severely criticized this type of behavior and it has mentioned that since these people have no power over one's destiny, then why should they behave in such a way? Such a thing is illogical and of no use to anyone!

---

[1] Biḥār al-Anwār, vol. 72, p. 300.

Lesson Eighteen
Envy

Tradition:

الْحَاسِدُ مُضِرٌّ بِنَفْسِهِ قَبْلَ أَنْ يَضُرَّ بِالْمَحْسُودِ

Imam Ṣādiq (ʻa) is narrated to have said: The envious one ends up harming himself before harming the object of his envy.[1]

Brief Commentary:

Envy is when someone cannot bear to see others enjoying various blessings and he attempts to remove those blessings from them through certain means or he tries to harm them in some way. In reality, an envious person is always trying to take things away from other people and not to progress himself in order to reach the rank and status that others have. There is no doubt that envy is a serious moral disease. From the perspective of psychology, an envious person ends up harming themselves more than the individual whom they are envious of. So it is better that such a person should try their best to grow and progress beyond what they see in others rather than simply trying to pull them backwards to their own level.

[1] Biḥār al-Anwār, vol. 73, p. 225.

Lesson Nineteen
The Ones Who Are Far From God's Mercy

Tradition:

مَنْ وَجَدَ مَاءً وَتُرَابًا ثُمَّ افْتَقَرَ فَأَبْعَدَهُ اللهُ

Imam 'Alī ('a) is narrated to have said: One who has land and water available to him and is poor and needy in spite of this, is verily far from the mercy of God.[1]

Brief Commentary:

From the Islamic sourcebooks, it is clear that Muslims must put to use all of the resources which they can possibly utilize, such as animal husbandry, farming, mining of underground resources, the establishment of factories, trade, etc... All of these things must be used to fight against poverty and even if a country only possesses one of these resources, they must utilize it to its full potential. If this one resource is properly utilized, then it's very possible that in time, all of the other resources can slowly develop and progress within the country. If an individual or a country fails to utilize these blessings, then they are truly far from God's mercy and the spirit of Islam. Islam has censured those who idly sit around and seek the aid of other people; this is especially true when one possesses the means and the wherewithal to grow and progress economically.

---

[1] Biḥār al-Anwār, vol. 103, p. 65.

Lesson Twenty
The Worst Friends

Tradition:

شَرُّ إِخْوَانِكَ مَنْ دَاهَنَكَ فِي نَفْسِكَ وَسَاتَرَكَ عَيْبَكَ

Imam 'Alī ('a) is narrated to have said: Your worst friends are those who flatter and praise you and hide from you your defects.[1]

Brief Commentary:

Fleeing from reality and covering the truth can never help us resolve the various issues that we face in our day to day lives. It is for this same reason that when our friends hide the realities they see within us, rather than helping us through constructive criticism, they are doing us the biggest disservice. Usually, this is done in order to gain the friend's favor or they see it as a positive attribute in and of itself, where one only mentions the good things about a friend, and where one hides all of the negative things. The truth is that such actions are actually disloyalty to one's friends and close ones, even if such people don't see it as such. In some cases, this brand of disloyalty ends up costing these friends dearly later on in life.

---

[1] Narrated from the book Ghurar al-Ḥikam.

Lesson Twenty One

The Completion of One's Actions

Tradition:

اسْتِتْمَامُ الْمَعْرُوفِ خَيْرٌ مِنِ ابْتِدَائِهِ

The Prophet (ṣ) is narrated to have said: Completing and following through with good actions is better and more important than simply initiating them.[1]

Brief Commentary:

In the sphere of our social lives, we oftentimes begin good actions which we later leave incompleted. In the beginning, there is a lot of eagerness towards the performance of such actions, but as time passes, we sometimes lose focus and leave the work partially finished. Islam prefers individuals who have faith and who are hard working towards their goals; whenever they begin something, they push through and finish it!

---

[1] Narrated from the book Nahj al-Faṣāḥah.

Lesson Twenty Two
Everlasting Plans

Tradition:

إِنَّ اللهَ لَمْ يَبْعَثْ نَبِيًّا إِلَّا بِصِدْقِ الْحَدِيثِ وَأَدَاءِ الْأَمَانَةِ

Imam Ṣādiq (ʻa) is narrated to have said: God ordered all of his prophets to invite the people of the world to truthfulness and the giving back of the trusts.[1]

Brief Commentary:

A healthy society is one that is based on various foundations and the most important of these is that of public trust. This includes trust related to speech and action; the biggest enemy to these two things is lying and treachery. If we look at a society where lying and treachery is commonly found, then we find that people fear one another and they feel alone and isolated. Everyone bears their burdens alone and this is a society of isolated and disconnected people. It is for this reason that inviting people to truthfulness and safeguarding what people have entrusted are important parts of the prophetic message as sent down by God.

[1] Narrated from the book Safīnat al-Biḥār.

Lesson Twenty Three
The Severest of Punishments

Tradition:

أَشَدُّ النَّاسِ عَذَابًا فِي الْقِيَامَةِ عَالِمٌ لَمْ يَنفَعْهُ عِلْمُهُ

The Prophet (ṣ) is narrated to have said: He who knows something and does not act upon it and benefit from his knowledge will be punished more severely than others on the Day of Judgment.[1]

Brief Commentary:

From Islam's perspective, knowledge is a tool used primarily for action. Knowledge is something that one uses to improve their personal life and the life of their society, and without such action, knowledge is of no value. Those who act based on a lack of knowledge have a lesser responsibility than those who know and still act improperly. When someone knows and acts improperly, then this is really a heavy responsibility which hangs upon their necks. Everyone is responsible to the same degree as the knowledge that they possess. The one who has more knowledge is duty-bound to apply this greater amount, while the one who has less knowledge is duty-bound to apply this lesser amount.

---

[1] Biḥār al-Anwār, vol. 2, p. 38.

Lesson Twenty Four
The Calamity of Debt

Tradition:

إِيَّاكُمْ وَالدَّيْنَ فَإِنَّهُ هَمٌّ بِاللَّيْلِ وَذُلٌّ بِالنَّهَارِ

The Holy Prophet (ṣ) is narrated to have said: Stay away from taking loans as much as possible, for it brings sorrow during the nights and it brings abjectness during the days.[1]

Brief Commentary:

The glitter of the modern-day lifestyle and the never ending race for gathering up newer and better things has caused a great number of people to place themselves into debt. Unfortunately, this debt is without any real need or purpose and it causes great difficulties in their lives. Someone who is indebted is not truly a free individual and we have been instructed in Islam not to take a loan unless there is a very real and severe need for it. When a country becomes indebted to another, this poses an even greater danger and its effects are more severe. Such debt causes one nation to become a slave to another and it chips away at its independence and freedom.

[1] Biḥār al-Anwār, vol. 103, p. 141.

LESSON TWENTY FIVE
A HEALTHY SOCIAL LIFE

Tradition:

لَو أَنَّ النَّاسَ أَدَّوْاْ حُقُوقَهُمْ لَكَانُواْ عَايِشِينَ بِخَيْرٍ

Imam Ṣādiq ('a) is narrated to have said: If the people were to honor the mutual rights of one another and to help those in need, then their lives would become pleasant and satisfying for them.[1]

Brief Commentary:

The aforementioned tradition is telling everyone that if the rights are attended to and the needy are taken care of, then the very quality of one's life will change for the better. This shows that the financial rights of the people cannot be considered just an ethical issue. It is in reality an important foundational aspect of social life which brings about widespread societal health and peace.

The dangerous situation that we have at hand today, where society has been divided into varying classes, shows how important this issue really is. As long as the people of this world believe that 'might makes right', this issue will never be resolved; people will have to understand that just because they are momentarily powerful, this does not allow them to take other people's rights away from them. This puts them and the society overall at great risk.

---

[1] Wasā'il al-Shī'ah, vol. 6, p. 2.

LESSON TWENTY SIX
THE KEY TO MISFORTUNE

Tradition:

إِنَّ اللهَ جَعَلَ لِلشَّرِّ أَقْفَالًا وَجَعَلَ مَفَاتِيحَ تِلْكَ الْأَقْفَالَ الشَّرَابَ، وَشَرٌّ مِنَ الشَّرَابِ الْكَذِبُ

Imam Ḥasan ʿAskarī (ʿa) is narrated to have said: God has created a lock for all the evils and the key to this lock is found in wine (alcohol). And lying is worse than wine![1]

Brief Commentary:

The greatest preventative factor against the evils found in this world is the faculty of the intellect. This is a most secure lock that has been placed upon these evils. This lock can easily be opened with the 'key' of alcohol, and once it has been opened, all of these evils come rushing out. When a person is in a drunken state, they will say and do almost anything, and even the greatest of sins do not seem so evil any longer.

Even though the drunken person commits sins due to a lack of proper judgment and thinking, the individual who lies with full awareness destroys the bonds that society has been established upon. When such trust is broken in the society, this gives rise to a great many sins, deviations, and widespread corruption. It is for this reason that lying is considered to be even more dangerous than alcohol.

---

[1] Wasāʾil al-Shīʿah, vol. 2, p. 223.

Lesson Twenty Seven

The Signs of those Bound for Heaven

Tradition:

لِأَهلِ الجَنَّةِ أَربَعُ عَلَامَاتٍ: وَجْهٌ مُنْبَسِطٌ، وَلِسانٌ فَصِيحٌ لَطِيفٌ، وَقَلْبٌ رَحِيمٌ، وَيَدٌ مُعطِيَةٌ

Imam Ṣādiq (ʻa) is narrated to have said: The people of paradise have four signs: A smiling and open face, an expressive tongue, a heart full of love and affection, and a generous and giving hand.[1]

Brief Commentary:

The most authentic religions are those which see human beings as the very heart of society and cause that society to give rise to valuable individuals. This is because the social sphere is the root of all spiritual and material blessings found on this earth. The aforementioned tradition has brought forward four signs of those who are heaven-bound. All of these signs are related to issues that are socially relevant and not anything which is of a worship-based nature.

The first sign is a relaxed and open face, which is full of joy and affection. The second is a tongue which expresses love and speaks goodly words to the people in a very clear and expressive way. The third sign is a heart which beats for other people, while the fourth is a hand which does not refrain from helping others. These are the signs of those who are heaven bound.

---

[1] From the book Irshād al-Qulūb.

Lesson Twenty Eight
The Signs of the Hypocrites

Tradition:

قَالَ لُقمَانُ لِابْنِهِ: لِلْمُنَافِقِ ثَلَاثُ عَلامَاتٍ:

يُخَالِفُ لِسانُهُ قَلْبَهُ، وَقَلْبُهُ فِعلَهُ، وَعَلانِيَتُهُ سَرِيرَتَهُ

Imam Ṣādiq ('a) is narrated to have said: Luqmān said to his son- The hypocrites have three signs: Their tongues are not in concordance with their hearts, and their hearts are not in concordance with their actions, and their outer is not in concordance with their inner.[1]

Brief Commentary:

Hypocrisy is a dangerous disease which arises from a deficiency of one's personality and a weakness of willpower. People who attempt to show themselves as something they are not and whose inner aspects do not match up with their outer aspects are typically weak people devoid of courage and willpower. They behave treacherously with others, as well as with themselves. There is no one more dangerous than them in the society because they manifest something which is nonexistent within themselves. They show a very beautiful outer appearance, but their inner reality is corrupt and polluted.

[1] Taken from the book Biḥār al-Anwār, vol. 15.

Lesson Twenty Nine
Taking Lesson and Guidance

Tradition:

اتَّعِظُوا بِمَنْ كَانَ قَبْلَكُم قَبْلَ أَنْ يَتَّعِظَ بِكُم مَنْ بَعدَكُمْ

Imam 'Alī ('a) is narrated to have said: Take lesson from your predecessors before those who proceed you take lesson from you.[1]

Brief Commentary:

History is full of lessons for humankind. It is full of guidance, words of wisdom, and good counsel. It is also full of examples of oppression, controversy, disunity, civilizational decline, and a lack of awareness toward one's environment and time period. In the midst of all this, Imam 'Alī ('a) is telling us to take lesson and guidance from the people who lived before us and not allow ourselves to become a lesson on how things should not be done by those who will come after us. Life will quickly pass all of us by and we must take advantage of the time that we have on this earth.

[1] Nahj al-Balāghah, Sermon 31.

Lesson Thirty
Speech and Silence

Tradition:

لَا خَيْرَ فِي الصَّمتِ عَنِ الحُكْمِ كَمَا أَنَّهُ لَا خَيْرَ فِي القَولِ بِالجَهلِ

Imam ʿAlī (ʿa) is narrated to have said: There is no benefit in the silence of the knowledgeable, just as there is no benefit in the speech of the ignorant.[1]

Brief Commentary:

God has taken a covenant from those who know that they should not remain silent when they see people committing sins, or when they witness deviations and other such similar things. They must use logic and reasoning in order to guide the people to the truth and towards justice. Everyone is responsible to the degree of their knowledge. Similarly, those who don't know should not interfere in such matters or else they will simply push the people into deviation. It is both wrong for the knowledgeable to be silent, just as it is wrong for the ignorant to speak in regards to what they do not know.

---

[1] Nahj al-Balāghah, Aphorisms.

Lesson Thirty One
The Pleasure of Forgiveness

Tradition:

إذا قَدَرْتَ عَلى عَدُوِّكَ فَاجْعَلِ العَفْوَ شُكراً لِلقُدرَةِ عَلَيهِ

The Prophet (ṣ) is narrated to have said: When you become victorious over your enemy, make forgiveness and pardon the tax that is due upon such a victory.[1]

Brief Commentary:

From the Islamic perspective, every blessing has its own kind of tax that is due and this is true without any exceptions. In line with this concept, the tax of power is forgiveness and pardon. Such a tax becomes due when the heart of the enemy is purified from the hatred and animosity that he previously held. When the original root of that opposition is eliminated, then that is the time when the tax must be paid.

When this forgiveness is freely given, the same individual who hated you yesterday will become your closest of friends today. It is at this time that true victory is achieved, where one is victorious both in the physical realm, as well as the inner and unseen realm. At the same time, those who quickly seek out revenge are not only deprived of this great virtue, but they also put their victory in danger as well.

---

[1] From the book: The Words of Muḥammad (ṣ).

Lesson Thirty Two

The True Meaning of Asceticism

Tradition:

الزَّاهِدُ فِي الدُّنْيَا مَنْ لَمْ يَغلِبِ الحَرامُ صَبْرَهُ، وَلَمْ يَشْغِلْ الحَلَالُ شُكْرَهُ

Imam ʿAlī (ʿa) is narrated to have said: The true ascetic in this world is he whose resistance (against what is unlawful) is not neutralized by the allure of unlawful wealth, while the lawful wealth does not take him away from the remembrance of God and his duty of being thankful towards him.[1]

Brief Commentary:

Some people have distorted the meaning of the term ascetic (Zāhid) and they have transformed the concept into a very negative form. They have redefined this term as referring to someone who distances themselves from all things material, and who steps away from all economic activities and lives like the needy and poverty stricken. This is while such a concept is an incorrect one and true asceticism is that which was lived by the Ahl al-Bayt themselves.

The aforementioned tradition can be divided into two main points. The first is that one must resist and close their eyes to all forms of unlawful wealth. The second is that one should never forget the responsibilities that come with lawful wealth. If we were to define asceticism in this manner, then this is an asceticism which is progressive and positive for the society at large. This is the opposite of false asceticism, which is undoubtedly a negative and destructive force for the society.

[1] From the book Tuḥaf al-ʿUqūl.

Lesson Thirty Three
Being of the Same Rank as the Martyrs

Tradition:

مَا الْمُجَاهِدُ الشَّهِيدُ فِي سَبِيلِ اللهِ بِأَعْظَمَ أَجْرًا مِمَّنْ قَدَرَ فَعَفَّ

Imam ʿAlī (ʿa) is narrated to have said: The one who fights in the way of God and is martyred is not greater than the one who had the ability to sin but kept himself pure.[1]

Brief Commentary:

According to Islam, the greatest struggle is the struggle that one performs against their own rebellious desires, and this is particularly true in a polluted social environment. Even when one is fighting against a dangerous enemy who seeks to destroy them, this fight will never be successful until the defenders possess sincerity, unity, and pure intentions. If the defenders are entangled with selfishness and disunity, they can never overcome their enemy.

It is for this same reason that Imam ʿAlī (ʿa) has mentioned that those who fight against their desires and lusts and keep themselves pure in a corrupt environment are no less in rank than those who are martyred fighting in the way of God. In the *Nahj al-Balāghah*, it has even been mentioned that such people are placed in the ranks of the heavenly angels.

[1] Narrated from the Nahj al-Balāghah, Aphorisms.

Lesson Thirty Four
The Best of the People

Tradition:

خَيْرُ النَّاسِ قُضَاةُ الْحَقِّ

Imam 'Alī ('a) is narrated to have said: The best of the people are those who judge in truth.[1]

Brief Commentary:

Proper judgment in issues related to the society, the law, and morality are only possible in a person who leaves aside his personal biases and grudges, and who looks out for the true interests of the people. Such a thing is only possible in someone who possesses the light of faith and human virtue. Furthermore, he must truly feel for the people in a way unaffected by personal interests and biases. These are the ones who are worthy of being considered the 'best of the people'.

[1] Taken from the book Islām Dar Qalbe Ijtimā' (Islam in the Heart of the Society).

LESSON THIRTY FIVE
THE WORSHIP OF THE FREE ONES

Tradition:

الْعُبَّادُ ثَلَاثَةٌ:

قَوْمٌ عَبَدُوا اللهَ – عَزَّ وَجَلَّ – خَوْفًا فَتِلكَ عِبَادَةُ العَبِيدِ

وَقَومٌ عَبَدُوا اللهَ – تَبَارَكَ وَتَعَالَى – طَلَبَ الثَّوَابِ فَتِلكَ عِبَادَةُ الْأُجَرَاءِ

وَقَومٌ عَبَدُوا اللهَ – عَزَّ وَجَلَّ – حُبًّا لَهُ فَتِلكَ عِبَادَةُ الأَحرارِ

Imam Ṣādiq ('a) is narrated to have said: The worshippers are of three groups. There are those who worship God out of fear of the hellfire, and this is the worship of the slaves. Then there are those who worship God for the rewards (which are offered), and this is the worship of the wage earners. Then there is the worship of those who worship God out of their love and affection for him and this is the worship of the free ones.[1]

Brief Commentary:

God's promise is true in that he will reward some and punish others based on their actions. His rewards will be extraordinary in scope, as will his punishment. In spite of this, the 'free ones' see through these rewards, looking at God alone. They seek nothing but God and they fill their heart only with his love. Their eyes are looking at something much higher than simply reward and punishment and their goal in life is to obey God. Thus they obey God out of their love and understanding of him.

---

[1] Taken from the book Wasā'il al-Shī'ah.

Lesson Thirty Six
What Breaks the Back!

Tradition:

ثَلَاثٌ قَاصِمَاتُ الظَّهرِ: رَجُلٌ استَكْثَرَ عَمَلَهُ وَنَسِيَ ذُنُوبَهُ وَأُعْجِبَ بِرَأيِهِ

Imam Bāqir (ʻa) is narrated to have said: There are three things which break a person's back: Counting one's good actions as being immense in scale, forgetting one's sins, and being obstinate in one's personal opinions.[1]

Brief Commentary:

Those who count their good deeds as being immense in scope will surely become satisfied with them, no matter how few or how small they happen to be. This acts as a preventative factor for further growth and progress. Those who forget their sins will soon commit new ones, until they have destroyed themselves. Those who only rely upon their own opinions are deprived of the collective intellects of their society. They are deprived of many forms of knowledge which others possess. As a result, they are soon overtaken by their mistakes and destroyed with the passing of time.

[1] Wasā'il al-Shīʻah, vol. 1, p. 73.

Lesson Thirty Seven

Be Pure!

Tradition:

أَفوَاهُكُمْ طَرِيقٌ مِنْ طُرُقِ رَبِّكُمْ فَأَحَبُّهَا إِلَى اللهِ أَطْيَبُهَا رِيحًا فَطَيِّبُوهَا بِمَا قَدَرْتُمْ عَلَيهِ

The Prophet (ṣ) is narrated to have said: Your mouths are one of the pathways towards God and the most beloved mouth in front of God is the one which is the best smelling. So make your mouths sweet smelling as much as possible.[1]

Brief Commentary:

This tradition, which has been narrated in the book Wasā'il al-Shī'ah, has both an inner meaning and an outer meaning in regards to brushing one's teeth. The outer meaning relates to the fact that we use our mouths to recite the remembrances of God, we recite the holy verses of the Quran, and we supplicate to him. Therefore, we must be careful to keep our mouths clean and pleasant smelling.

The inner meaning of this tradition is referring to the fact that our mouths are one of the ways through which we can connect to God. It is a means of connection between God and his servants. The further we keep our mouths away from lying, slander, anger, and other such negative forces, the more beloved we become to God. The purer our mouths become, the more loved we are by God!

---

[1] Wasā'il al-Shī'ah, vol. 1, p. 358.

Lesson Thirty Eight
The End Results of Ignorance

Tradition:

مَنْ عَمِلَ عَلَى غَيرِ عِلْمٍ أَفْسَدَ أَكْثَرَ مِمّا يُصْلِحُ

Imam Jawād ('a) is narrated to have said: He who acts without knowledge and awareness will destroy more than what he fixes.[1]

Brief Commentary:

The cost of ignorance isn't only that human beings will not reach the true meaning and full value of their lives; rather, much corruption and destructive acts also result from it as well. In such a case for example, an individual may intend to help their child, but they will only hurt them. They may want to serve the cause of Islam and humanity, but they will only disgrace the religion and the human race. They may want to resolve a conflict that has erupted, but they will only make things worse. In everything that they do, they make things worse, rather than make them better.

---

[1] Muntahī al-Āmāl.

LESSON THIRTY NINE
THE FOUNDATIONS OF GUIDANCE

Tradition:

الْمُؤْمِنُ يَحتَاجُ إلَى ثَلَاثِ خِصَالٍ:

تَوفِيقٍ مِنَ اللهِ

وَوَاعِظَةٍ مِنْ نَفْسِهِ

وَقَبُولٍ مِمَنْ يَنْصَحُهُ

Imam Jawād (ʻa) is narrated to have said: Faithful believers are in need of three things: Divine favor, counsel which arises from the heart, and the acceptance of other people's advice.[1]

Brief Commentary:

Human beings tread a path that is full of ups and downs, and which possesses many dangers. In order to transform oneself into an effective and beneficial member of society, one must first develop a spiritual connection with his Lord. This connection will awaken his conscience within him, which will in turn guide and advise him in his day to day affairs. In addition to this inner voice which guides him, such a person will also need to listen to the advice and counsel of others as well, in order that he may walk on the best path possible.

---

[1] Muntahī al-Āmāl.

LESSON FORTY

THE LAMENTATION OF IGNORANCE

Tradition:

مِمَّا حَدَّثَ بِهِ رَسُولُ الله (صلَّى الله عليه وآله) وَلَم يَسبِقْهُ أَحَدٌ لِقَوْلِهِ: النِّيَاحَةُ مِنْ عَمَلِ الْجَاهِلِيَّةِ

Imam Bāqir ('a) is narrated to have reported a saying of the Prophet (ṣ) which no one had mentioned before him. He said: Lamentations are one of the actions from the era of ignorance (the time of the Jāhilīyah). (This means that when we are faced with problems in life, we should not simply sit down and cry about them. Rather, we should stand up and go towards resolving the issue at hand!)[1]

Brief Commentary:

This tradition is brief but it contains both an inner and an outer meaning. The outer meaning pertains to the actions which people used to perform and were prevalent during the time of ignorance (the era before Islam). When someone would pass away, the women would begin crying and lamenting his death in a way where they would say false things about the individual. So in reality, they would make up lies about the person and this was a false form of mourning.

Another possible meaning which Imam Bāqir ('a) may have intended is that when one faces personal or social problems, lamenting over them is useless and a waste of time and energy. Instead of sitting down and crying over our problems, we should rather utilize our intellects and be persistent in resolving whatever issue has come about.

---

[1] Wasā'il al-Shī'ah, vol. 1, p. 915.

Lesson Forty One
Account for Your Actions Every Day

Tradition:

لَيْسَ مِنَّا مَنْ لَمْ يُحَاسِبْ نَفْسَهُ كُلَّ يَوْمٍ

Imam Kāẓim ('a) is narrated to have said: He who does not account (his actions) each day is not from us![1]

Brief Commentary:

The only possible way to prevent harm to ourselves and work towards further progress is to sit down each day and account for all of what we have done and said. Growth is not possible except through such detailed accounting and this includes both the young, as well as the old. It is actually surprising that people will spend so much time accounting for their financial state, and they spend so much time looking after their physical well being, yet when it comes to their ethical and spiritual accounting, they are completely negligent. It's possible for someone to spend virtually no time accounting for their spiritual state during the span of their entire lifetime. This is an extremely frightening state of being.

On the other hand, a responsible and aware Muslim is one who lives by the words of Imam Kāẓim ('a) in the aforementioned tradition. He always accounts for the actions and deeds of every single day. If he has done something good, he attempts to further it in scope, and if he has done something bad, he asks God to forgive him for his lapse. Over a lifetime, such accounting will increase the good that one does and decrease the evil significantly.

[1] From the book Aqwāl al-A'immah, vol. 1, p. 214.

Lesson Forty Two

Faith is Harder and Stronger than Iron

Tradition:

إِنَّ الْمُؤمِنَ أَشَدُّ مِنْ زُبُرِ الْحَدِيد؛ إِنَّ زُبُرَ الحَدِيدِ إِذَا أُدْخِلَ النّارَ تَغَيَّرَ، وَإِنَّ الْمُؤْمِنَ لَو قُتِلَ ثُمَّ نُشِرَ ثُمَّ قُتِلَ لَمْ يَتَغَيَّرْ قَلْبُهُ

Imam Ṣādiq (ʻa) is narrated to have said: People with faith are stronger than pieces of iron for when iron is placed into a fire, it changes, but if the believers are killed, brought back to life, and then killed again, no change will be found in their hearts.[1]

Brief Commentary:

Life is composed of various difficulties and complicated issues. People who have weak levels of resistance are quickly brought down to their knees in the face of these issues. Yet those who have strong faith are filled with a spirit of resistance and perseverance. Such people will never surrender in the face of these difficulties and they will persevere until the very end.

People who possess faith understand that when one is walking on the path of obedience to God, away from all types of sins, then such a path will naturally have its share of problems and difficulties. Anything worthwhile in life has its own share of difficulties and cannot be easily reached. One must be prepared with a spirit of hard work, perseverance, and self sacrifice in order to reach such high ranks. One must stand up against their own rebellious desires, and by standing firm against these issues, one will be victorious in the end.

[1] From the book Safīnat al-Biḥār, vol. 1, p. 37.

Lesson Forty Three
The Reality of Monotheism and Divine Justice

Tradition:

التَّوحِيدُ أَنْ لَا تَتَوَهَّمَهُ، وَالْعَدْلُ أَنْ لَا تَتَّهِمَهُ

Imam ʻAlī (ʻa) is narrated to have said: The reality of God's oneness is that you should not limit his essence to your imagination, and faith in his justice is that you should not accuse him in regards to anything.[1]

Brief Commentary:

God's existence is clear and manifest for us in this world and even the smallest things are a reminder and a proof of his greatness. At the same time, the reality of his essence (Dhāt) is hidden to us because he is an existence without any limitations and therefore, he is higher than our limited understanding. Due to this reason, we must consider his essence to be higher than anything which we can possibly imagine.

The second issue discussed in this tradition is God's justice and it has been explained that everything which takes place in this world happens based on precise rules and due to very exact reasons. Therefore, we should never look at anything which happens with a negative point of view and imagine that God has done something improper or wrong. Such a view of God is not in concordance with faith and belief in his perfection.

[1] Nahj al-Balāghah, Aphorisms.

Lesson Forty Four
Several Signs of Faith

Tradition:

الْمُؤْمِنُ حَسَنُ الْمَعُونَةِ، خَفِيفُ الْمَؤُنَةِ، جَيِّدُ التَّدْبِيرِ لِمَعِيشَتِهِ، لَا يُلْسَعُ مِنْ جُحْرٍ مَرَّتَيْنِ

Imam Ṣādiq (ʻa) is narrated to have said: A believing individual's help is valuable, his expenses are little, he lives prudently (living according to plan), and he is never bitten from the same hole twice.[1]

Brief Commentary:

Faith has various signs which can be intellectual, moral, or social in nature. This tradition has mentioned four such signs which are present in those who have faith. The first sign states that those who have faith help their brothers and are very valuable to them. The reason behind this is that those who have faith act based on love, awareness, and complete sincerity towards their brothers. This type of help is exponentially greater than help based on other motivations.

The second sign is that such people live a simple lifestyle far away from show and ostentation. Such lifestyles naturally bring about pressure which causes people to engage in sinful behavior in order to reach their financial goals. The third sign is that such people live their lives according to plan and this also relates to financial matters as well. The fourth sign is that whenever something goes wrong, they quickly learn their lessons and due to this reason, they never receive two blows from the same source.

---

[1] Taken from the book Safīnat al-Biḥār.

Lesson Forty Five

The Worldly Life is Not the Goal- - It is Simply the Means!

Tradition:

الدُّنْيا خُلِقَتْ لِغَيْرِها وَلَمْ تُخلَقْ لِنَفْسِهَا

Imam ʿAlī (ʿa) is narrated to have said: The world has been created for another purpose and not for its own sake.[1]

Brief Commentary:

Some people become confused when they see some verses of the Quran and various traditions praising the world and mentioning how it is the 'marketplace or the agricultural field of the saints', while other sources mention the complete opposite, censuring the world and considering it a dangerous and deceptive phenomenon. Such verses and traditions seem to be in contradiction with one another.

Yet this tradition clears up this misunderstanding and explains that if the world is taken as a means for reaching human perfection and growth, then it becomes something positive and beloved. At the same time, if it becomes an end in itself and the means of sin, arrogance, and rebellion against God, then it becomes the most hated and dangerous thing possible.

---

[1] From Safīnat al-Biḥār, vol. 1.

Lesson Forty Six
The Value of Human Beings

Tradition:

إِنَّهُ لَيْسَ لِأَنْفُسِكُمْ ثَمَنٌ إِلَّا الْجَنَّةُ فَلَا تَبِيعُوهَا إِلَّا بِهَا

Imam ʿAlī (ʿa) is narrated to have said: Know that you are worthy of nothing but the everlasting felicity of paradise and so you shouldn't sell yourself for anything less.[1]

Brief Commentary:

If someone was asked how much they considered their life was worth, they would typically consider it as being priceless. The reality is that our lives are so precious we can't even fathom an amount we would be willing to sell it for. Unfortunately, the truth is that most people sell their lives for things of meager value every single day. At the end of their lives, they see that they have given away their lives for something like a house, a car, or a boat. Such people have in reality exchanged the very essence of their lives for things of little to no value. Interestingly enough, they realize that they must soon leave even these inconsequential things which they have exchanged the long years of their lives for.

Here Imam ʿAlī (ʿa) is telling us that there is nothing in this world that is worth our souls. There is nothing that we can gain in this world that is worth the value of our lives. The only thing which is worth this grand amount is the pleasure of God and the perfection and completion of ourselves as human beings. Even if we were to exchange the entirety of our lives for the pleasure of God and the reward of paradise, it would be well worth it. In fact, such an exchange is the only thing which can be considered a proper trade for our life's work.

[1] Nahj al-Balāghah, Aphorism 456.

Lesson Forty Seven
Truth and Falsehood

Tradition:

إِنَّ الْحَقَّ ثَقِيلٌ مَرِيءٌ، وإِنَّ الْبَاطِلَ خَفِيفٌ وَبِيءٌ

Imam ʻAlī (ʻa) is narrated to have said: The truth is heavy and difficult, yet it is refreshing and agreeable, while falsehood is light and easy, yet it is painful and dangerous.[1]

Brief Commentary:

This description of truth and falsehood by Imam ʻAlī (ʻa) is extremely brief in terms of words but it is at the same time exceedingly eloquent. The tradition mentions that while truth may initially seem abrasive and harsh, it is in reality something quite wholesome and agreeable for the people. Truth is something which is healthy and necessary for the society at large.

At the same time, falsehood is so easy to spread and it can even seem pleasurable to the one's spreading it and to the ones hearing it. It can easily be compared to a delicious type of food that is in actuality poison. It may taste good when one is taking those first bites, but as soon as the body begins to absorb it, it shows its true nature and destroys the person completely.

[1] Biḥār al-Anwār, vol. 70, p. 107.

Lesson Forty Eight

The Most Valuable Legacy of the Arabs

Tradition:

أَصدَقُ كَلِمةٍ قَالَتْها العَرَبُ كَلِمَةُ لَبيدٍ حَيْثُ قَالَ:

أَلَا كُلُّ شَيْءٍ مَا خَلَا اللهَ باطِلُ وَكُلُّ نَعِيمٍ لَا مَحَالَةَ زَائِلُ

The Prophet (ṣ) is narrated to have said: The most correct and far reaching sentence which the Arabs have mentioned can be found in the words of Lubayd (a famous Arab poet) when he said: Know that everything except God is void and useless and every blessing will eventually slip through your hands.[1]

Brief Commentary:

The finite nature of wealth and social position, as well as their inevitable loss, teaches us that we should be careful to earn them in lawful and just ways, and we should also be careful to spend them in moderate and lawful ways. We should understand that the only infinite existence is that of God and we all exist due to his mercy. This thought should be enough to keep us humble while we are living the life of this world.

---

[1] Miṣbāḥ al-Sharī'ah, p. 45.

Lesson Forty Nine
I am Weary and Disgusted of Them

Tradition:

لَيْسَ مِنَّا مَنْ غَشَّ مُسْلِمًا أَوْ ضَرَّهُ أو ماكَرَهُ

Imam Riḍā ('a) is narrated to have said: He who cheats, harms, or tricks another Muslim is not from us.[1]

Brief Commentary:

Those who find happiness in other people's misfortunes and consider their own benefit to be in such things cannot be considered as true Muslims; rather, they can't even be considered proper human beings. What makes human beings superior to other animals can be found in their social behavior and the individual who seeks their benefit in the harm of others is lacking in this social aspect.

In some cases, people may try to harm others openly and in a direct fashion, and in other cases they may attempt to do so quietly and in a hidden fashion. Islam has forbidden all such types of behavior which harms others. Imam Riḍā ('a) has said: I am a stranger to those who commit such actions.

---

[1] Safīnat al-Biḥār, Ghash (adulteration).

Lesson Fifty

The Efforts of the Weak

Tradition:

الغِيْبَةُ جُهْدُ العاجِزِ

Imam 'Alī ('a) is narrated to have said: Backbiting is the last resort of the weak individuals.[1]

Brief Commentary:

Amongst the greater sins, there are few sins like backbiting which manifest an individual's weakness and wretched nature. Those who sit around censuring and seeking out the faults of others (behind their backs) are in reality busy destroying the people's reputations and making people's faults public, which would have remained private. The fact of the matter is that most people are not without fault and it is likely that everyone has some point of weakness which they suffer from.

The question remains as to why anyone would behave in such a manner? The answer is that these people act in this way in order to soothe their feelings of jealousy and enmity which they hold against others. The only people who would engage in such a behavior are those who are so weak that they cannot even strike out at the people in a direct fashion and they resort to these cowardly means of hurting others. They are only capable of stabbing people in the back by constantly backbiting them. It has been mentioned in the traditions that if the one who backbites ends up repenting, then he will be the last of the people to enter paradise, and if he does not repent, then he will be the first of those who will enter the hellfire.

---

[1] Nahj al-Balāghah, Aphorisms.

Lesson Fifty One
The Signs of the Oppressors

Tradition:

لِلظَّالِمِ مِنَ الرِّجَالِ ثَلَاثُ عَلَامَاتٍ:
يَظْلِمُ مَنْ فَوْقَهُ بِالْمَعْصِيَةِ
وَمَنْ دُونَهُ بِالْغَلَبَةِ
وَيُظَاهِرُ الْقَوْمَ الظَّلَمَةِ

Imam ʿAlī (ʿa) is narrated to have said: An oppressor has three signs- He oppresses those who are above him through opposition and disobedience, he oppresses those who are below him through domination and compulsion, and he cooperates with the oppressors.[1]

Brief Commentary:

The one who possesses a spirit of oppression will always exhibit facets of this type of behavior through his actions. When he is supposed to obey the commands of those above him, he rebels and disobeys them. When he finds people who are employed by him or are under his command, he acts in a forceful way with them and puts them under pressure. The third sign is that he cooperates and collaborates with those who are oppressors as well. You will find that his friends and close associates all possess the characteristic of oppression. In a nutshell, such an individual is an oppressor in all aspects of his life and character, and it can clearly be seen that the attribute of oppression has taken over his entire being.

---

[1] Nahj al-Balāghah, Aphorisms.

Lesson Fifty Two

There is No Disease without a Cure

Tradition:

مَا أَنْزَلَ اللهُ مِنْ دَاءٍ إِلَّا جَعَلَ لَهُ دَوَاءً

The Prophet (ṣ) is narrated to have said: God has not created any pain (or disease) except that he also created its cure.[1]

Brief Commentary:

The world that we live in is composed of various actions and reactions, and everything which lies on one extreme possesses a relationship with something which lies on the other extreme. For example, when we have the phenomenon of cold in this world, there also exists warmth and heat. When there is anger, there is also calm. In this same way, there is a cure to be found for every disease that exists; the only issue is it must be sought out and found, just as a warm blanket is sought out in the face of the cold.

This doesn't only apply to problems of the physical body; it also applies to social and spiritual problems as well. Some people believe that various things are unsolvable and so when they see an issue, they just leave it alone, thinking that it must be tolerated with no way possible towards its resolution. These people are negligent of the reality that every pain and every disease possesses its own cure and in fact, there is no disease which cannot be cured in this world, be it physical, mental, emotional, social, or spiritual. Therefore, we must persevere and work hard when faced with the pains and problems of life and seek a way towards their resolution and cure.

---

[1] Nahj al-Faṣāḥah.

Lesson Fifty Three
What Neutralizes the Blessings?

Tradition:

إِنَّ اللهَ قَضَى قَضَاءً حَتْمًا أَلَّا يُنْعِمَ عَلَى الْعَبْدِ بِنِعْمَةٍ فَيَسْلُبَهَا إِيَّاهُ حَتَّى يُحْدِثَ الْعَبْدُ ذَنْبًا يَسْتَحِقُّ بِذٰلِكَ النِّقْمَةَ

Imam Bāqir (ʻa) is narrated to have said: God has made a decisive rule that he will never take away a blessing which he has given to the people unless they commit a sin which causes the loss of that blessing.[1]

Brief Commentary:

The blessings of God are without end but it cannot be said that they are without calculation and accounting. God never gives to the people without proper calculation and he never takes away from them without cause as well. When the people begin to use the blessings of God as a means of corruption, arrogance, and oppression, then those same blessings are transformed into the means for their destruction. It is at this time that that blessing is removed and a calamity comes in its place.

When such a thing happens, things like industry and technology (which are positive phenomenons) are turned into destructive elements. The society begins to fall apart and such blessings become the means for worry and anxiety. Even things which help the people and allow them to do things more efficiently become the means for their regression. This is all caused by the improper use of God's divine blessings.

---

[1] Uṣūl al-Kāfī, vol. 2.

Lesson Fifty Four
Martyrdom and Purity

Tradition:

إِذَا مُتَّ عَلَى طَهَارَةٍ تَكُونُ شَهِيدًا

The Prophet (ṣ) is narrated to have said: If you leave this world in a state of purity, you will be counted as being amongst the martyrs.[1]

Brief Commentary:

This tradition is a part of the commands which the Prophet (ṣ) gave to one of his companions by the name of Anas. He said to him: If you are able to be in a state of purity (Wuḍū) day and night, then do so. This is because if you were to leave this world in such a state then you would be a martyr. The tradition is primarily referring to the state of ritual purity known as Wuḍū but it also refers to a more important reality and that is the living of a pure life and the dying of a pure death.

Those whose thoughts, bodies, and lives are pure and they end up dying in this state are without any doubt amongst the ranks of the martyrs. Other traditions from the Ahl al-Bayt have also emphasized this reality.

[1] Safīnat al-Biḥār, vol. 1, p. 720.

Lesson Fifty Five
The Self Sacrificing Lovers

Tradition:

إِنَّ أَصْحَابَ جَدِّيَ الْحُسَيْنِ لَمْ يَجِدُوا أَلَمَ مَسِّ الْحَدِيدِ

Imam Bāqir (ʻa) is narrated to have said: The self sacrificing companions of my grandfather Imam Ḥusayn (ʻa) did not feel any pain under the striking of the swords and the piercing of the spears of the enemy.[1]

Brief Commentary:

When an individual begins to love something intensely, all of his senses will be focused on the object of his love. It is for this reason that any difficulty that he faces will be considered as nothing at all; in reality, he won't even feel any of these difficulties while he is in this state. When the women of Egypt saw Prophet Joseph (ʻa), they all cut their hands under the effect of this attraction and love. They became so taken in that they couldn't even feel themselves cutting deep into their hands, while this is something that should have caused them immense pain under normal conditions.

This shows that those who are taken in by the love of God and are willing to sacrifice themselves in his way will not feel the immense pain of the swords or bullets of the enemy as they strike into them. One must first love in this path and then the attributes of self sacrifice and endurance will follow!

[1] Biḥār al-Anwār, vol. 45, p. 80.

Lesson Fifty Six

The Wise and the Foolish

Tradition:

الْعَاقِلُ يَعْتَمِدُ عَلَى عَمَلِهِ وَالْجَاهِلُ يَعْتَمِدُ عَلَى أَمَلِهِ

Imam 'Alī ('a) is narrated to have said: The wise lean upon their hard work and actions while the foolish lean upon their hopes and desires.[1]

Brief Commentary:

People with wisdom live based on a code of positivity and the seeking of the truth, and it is for this reason that they go after their goals with solid planning and they don't simply rely on their imagination and dreams. Since it's not possible to reach such goals without hard work and struggle, one must truly persevere and be constant in their efforts.

The foolish on the other hand sit around floating in their dreams and hopes. They don't put any effort forward and they only imagine the things that they want to do and who they want to be. They gain pleasure out of these thoughts and since there is no effort required for conjuring up such ideas, they never end up doing anything. In spite of this, they are always in expectation of 'victory' over their imaginary goals, but without hard work and effort, they will never be able to achieve any of their dreams.

[1] Ghurar al-Ḥikam.

Lesson Fifty Seven
The Truly Religious Are Few in Number

Tradition:

النَّاسُ عَبِيدُ الدُّنْيَا، وَالدِّينُ لَعِقٌ عَلَى أَلْسِنَتِهِم يَحُوطُونَهُ مَا دَرَّتْ بِهِ مَعَايِشُهُم،
فَإِذَا مُحِّصُوا بِالبَلاءِ قَلَّ الدَّيَّانُونَ

Imam Ḥusayn (ʿa) is narrated to have said: Many of the people are slaves of this world and religion is something present only upon their tongues. As long as their lives are going well under the protection of their religion, they support it, but on the day when difficulties come about and they are tested, the truly religious are few in number.[1]

Brief Commentary:

Religion, particularly the religion of Islam, is a protector of the rights of the people in society. It supports what is truly in their best interests and it enacts justice in the society at large. In some situations, religion can go against the actual personal interests of various people. It is here that the truly religious and those who simply are posing as being religious are recognized and distinguished.

What we mean by this is that some people are only after their own personal interests and they are only religious as long as it benefits them materially. As soon as upholding the religion becomes a cause for material loss, they completely leave it. The truly religious are those who are loyal to their religion irregardless of whether it is to their material benefit or loss at that point in time. Faith is the major driving force of their lives and not personal material interest.

---

[1] Biḥār al-Anwār, vol. 10, p. 198.

Lesson Fifty Eight

Justice and Fairness Amongst One's Children

Tradition:

اعْدِلُوا بَيْنَ أَوْلَادِكُمْ كَمَا تُحِبُّونَ أَنْ يَعْدِلُوا بَيْنَكُمْ

The Prophet (ṣ) is narrated to have said: Be fair when it comes to your children just as you would like them to be fair when it comes to you.[1]

Brief Commentary:

A major problem amongst people is that they make differences between their children. In some families, the eldest child is treated differently and considered as being superior to the others. In some other cases, the youngest child is treated as being better than the rest. In these cases, the parents give all of their love, affection, and care to one of their children and create differences in how the rest are treated. This gives rise to anger and animosity amongst the siblings and they become enemies of one another. In addition, they hold some grudges against their parents as well, and this anger can also be directed towards the society at large.

[1] Biḥār al-Anwār, vol. 23.

Lesson Fifty Nine
You Are Always Being Watched!

Tradition:

اِعْلَمْ أَنَّكَ لَنْ تَخْلُوَ مِن عَيْنِ اللهِ فَانْظُرْ كَيْفَ تَكُونُ

Imam Jawād (ʿa) is narrated to have said: Know that you are never outside the sight of God, so be careful of how you behave![1]

Brief Commentary:

The first effect of faith in God is a feeling of constantly being under his watch. This isn't just a sense of physically being watched, but it also relates to one's inner state such as one's thoughts, feelings, and intentions. There is nothing that he does not see and this is the most comprehensive sense of being seen that could possibly exist.

As one's faith grows stronger, the sense of this observation also increases, becoming more comprehensive and deeper in scope. This continues until an individual sees themselves as being perpetually under watch! This state is the greatest and most powerful means of self and social reformation, and it is the most beautiful manifestation of faith. This is also the state which can cure the worst social ills present in our society today.

[1] Taken from the book Tuḥaf al-ʿUqūl.

Lesson Sixty

Neither Envy, Nor Flattery

Tradition:

الثَّناءُ بِأَكْثَرَ مِنَ الِاسْتِحْقَاقِ مَلَقٌ، وَالتَّقْصِيرُ عَنِ الِاسْتِحْقَاقِ عَيٌّ أَوْ حَسَدٌ

Imam ʿAlī (ʿa) is narrated to have said: Praising someone beyond what they are worthy of is flattery and praising them less than what they deserve is either an inability to express oneself or it is envy.[1]

Brief Commentary:

There is no doubt that we should praise those who perform worthy actions or possess worthy attributes. Such people should be encouraged in the path that they have chosen and they should be given this support. At the same time, this must be done in the correct manner and in the correct amount. If it is done excessively, then it is considered to be flattery and this is something which brings down the narrator's character and it also causes the rise of egoism and conceit in the one being praised. If such an action is performed less than what the person is worthy of then it also has negative consequences because the individual becomes discouraged and it is a sign of either envy or an inability of one to express themselves.

[1] Nahj al-Balāghah, Aphorisms.

Lesson Sixty One

Be in the Service of Your Brothers

Tradition:

مَنْ كَانَ فِي حَاجَةِ أَخِيهِ الْمُسْلِمُ كَانَ اللهُ فِي حَاجَتِهِ

Imam Ṣādiq (ʻa) is narrated to have said: He who helps fulfill the needs of his religious brothers will find that God will help him in fulfilling his needs.[1]

Brief Commentary:

People typically think that if they were to help others to resolve their problems, then they would fall behind and not progress within their own lives. Islam has explained that the reality is other than this and the Prophet (ṣ) in the aforementioned tradition has explained to us that if we help our brothers in religion, then God will in turn help us with the problems that we face. God is the one who holds true power and he is able to help us with any issue that we have. This is something which many have experienced in their own lives as well. Whenever they help others overcome their problems, they are helped in resolving theirs. In some cases, this help comes in strange and unexpected ways, and there is no doubt that this is a form of divine mercy and help.

---

[1] Biḥār al-Anwār, vol. 74, p. 286.

Lesson Sixty Two
Mistakes in Life

Tradition:

لَا تُشْعِرْ قَلْبَكَ الْهَمَّ عَلَى مَا فَاتَ فَيُشْغِلُكَ عمَّا هُوَ آتٍ

Imam 'Alī ('a) is narrated to have said: Do not busy your heart with sorrow over what has passed or else you will not be sufficiently prepared over what is to come (in the future).[1]

Brief Commentary:

There are very few people who haven't committed any mistakes in their lives or who haven't had missed opportunities. At this junction, people can be divided into two main groups: There are those who are always sorrowful over what has taken place in the past and the things that they have missed out on; they expend a great deal of energy reminiscing over what could have been. The second group is composed of those who consider what is past to be past and they basically let go of what took place beforehand, only taking lesson from these events for their future. They then mobilize all of their energy and power towards building their today and their future life. There is no doubt that the best method of living is in what Imam 'Alī ('a) has mentioned in the aforementioned tradition.

[1] Narrated from Ghurar al-Ḥikam, p. 289.

Lesson Sixty Three
Islam as the Religion of the World

Tradition:

لَا يَبْقَى عَلَى ظَهْرِ الْأَرْضِ بَيْتُ مَدَرٍ وَلَا وَبَرٍ إِلَّا أَدْخَلَهُ اللهُ كَلِمَةَ الْإِسْلَامِ

The Prophet (ṣ) of Islam is narrated to have said: There will be left no home on this earth, even homes made of earth or the woolen tents, except that God will have allowed Islam to enter within them.[1]

Brief Commentary:

Every day it is becoming more manifest that the religion of Islam is the best religion on the face of this earth. People are realizing that either they must leave religion completely aside or they must accept Islam as the true and final religion sent down by God. Since religion is an integral part of human nature and our intrinsic selves, it follows that people can't simply leave aside religion altogether. The only real option that they have left amongst the various religions is that of Islam. This phenomenon is manifested in our modern day world by the ever increasing rates of people accepting Islam as their faith and way of life. Islam has spread to virtually every nation on this earth and mosques can be found even in various far flung regions and cities.

With this said, it must be mentioned that the completion of this transformation will only take place with the appearance of Imam Mahdī (ʿa). On that day, polytheism and idol worship will be completely destroyed and Islam will manifest itself all throughout the world. This is the reality which the Prophet (ṣ) has given glad tidings of in the above tradition.

---

[1] Majmaʿ al-Bayān, Commentary on Surah Tawbah.

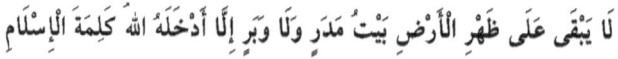

Lesson Sixty Four

Do Not Consider Any Sin as Being Small in Nature

Tradition:

مِنَ الذُّنُوبِ الَّتِي لَا تُغْفَرُ: لَيْتَنِي لَا أُؤَاخَذُ إِلَّا بِهٰذَا

Imam Ḥasan ʻAskarī (ʻa) is narrated to have said: Among the sins that will not be forgiven is the sin where an individual says: How I wish this was my only sin![1]

Brief Commentary:

In Islam, lesser sins can be transformed into greater sins and one such way is when they are considered as being small and inconsequential in nature. This is in fact one of the dangerous insinuations which Satan can make to man and he tells people that their sins are actually nothing to worry about because they are of no account. Greater sins which create fear in people and cause worry and anxiety are not as dangerous because the individual is always careful in regards to them and works hard to stay away from them.

Yet, as soon as someone looks at certain sins as being small in nature, their fear quickly leaves them and they become liable to commit them from time to time (or they may begin to commit them often). When such sins are committed repeatedly, they are then transformed into greater sins. Such sins are the cause of great torment and difficulty for the people, both in this world and in the next. They become greater sins because in a way, one is breaking the sanctity of God by repeatedly and purposely disobeying him and performing what he has made forbidden.

[1] Tuḥaf al-ʻUqūl, p. 366.

Lesson Sixty Five
The Superiority of Knowledge

Tradition:

فَضْلُ الْفَقِيهِ عَلَى الْعَابِدِ كَفَضْلِ الشَّمْسِ عَلَى الْكَوَاكِبِ

Imam Kāẓim ('a) is narrated to have said: The superiority of the scholar over the worshipper is like the superiority of the sun in relation to the stars.[1]

Brief Commentary:

The stars that are found in the skies possess light in and of themselves but they are not able to illuminate much else besides themselves. For example, their light is not able to illuminate our homes and our walkways on this earth. At the same time, the sun is so powerful that its rays illuminate the earth and all of that which exists upon it. It not only possesses intrinsic light, but it also lights the way for billions of human beings, as well as other creatures. This is a light which completely illuminates the roads for us and shows us where we need to go in our lives.

This metaphor can aptly be applied to the differences between a scholar who possesses knowledge and a worshipper who is devout but lacks this knowledge. The worshipper is only attempting to save himself but the scholar is one who is attempting to save countless numbers of individuals. This is truly a monumental difference between these two categories of believers. We should also keep in mind that if it were not for the scholars, then the worshippers could not exist either. It is through the light of the scholars that people are able to find their way and become devout worshippers of God.

---

[1] Tuḥaf al-'Uqūl, p. 307.

Lesson Sixty Six
Mutual Rights

Tradition:

يَلْزَمُ الْوَالِدَيْنِ مِنَ الْحُقُوقِ لِوَلَدِهِمَا مَا يَلْزَمُ الْوَلَدَ لَهُمَا مِنْ حُقُوقِهِمَا

The Prophet (ṣ) is narrated to have said: Just as the children are responsible if they don't uphold the rights of their mothers and fathers, the mothers and fathers are also responsible if they do not uphold the rights of their children.[1]

Brief Commentary:

In this world, wherever we find a right that has been enjoined, we will also find a responsibility which has been attached to it. Rights and responsibilities have been created alongside one another, and as the rights are greater in scope, so the responsibilities are heavier in relation as well. Just as parents have a great right upon their children (a right mentioned in the Quran as being of the same rank to the right that God has upon us), similarly, the children also have a great right upon their parents.

Parents must never be negligent of teaching and educating their children, not even for a moment. They must do everything possible in order to build up their children physically and spiritually, and protect them from intellectual and ethical corruption. The busyness and entanglement of day to day life is no excuse and it should not prevent the parents from performing their great responsibilities towards their children.

[1] Narrated from the book Aqwāl al-Aʿimmah.

Lesson Sixty Seven
Spend in the Way of God's Obedience So That You Do Not Spend In the Way of Sin!

Tradition:

إيّاكَ أَنْ تَمْنَعَ فِي طاعَةِ الله فَتَنْفُقَ مِثْلَيهِ فِي مَعْصِيَةِ الله

Imam Kāẓim ('a) is narrated to have said: Do not abstain from spending money in the way of God's obedience, for if you do, you will inevitably spend twice as much in the way of sin and error![1]

Brief Commentary:

There are some people who are so stingy when it comes to money that even when they become ill, they refuse to spend anything in treating themselves. As a result, their condition worsens and they later become forced to spend two or three times that amount in curing their sickness. This is in fact a general rule that if someone doesn't spend the necessary money on their basic expenses, they will in turn be forced to spend much more when an issue comes up later on.

Those who refrain from spending time or money for the education and training of their children will end up paying a back breaking price later on in life. Such neglect can bring out issues in their children like deviancy, criminality, and drug addiction. The parents will end up suffering a hundred fold for their initial neglect (which could have been remedied with just a small amount of time and effort). Similarly, if a person neglects to help the poverty stricken of their society, they will end up paying several times more to prevent various things which arise from that exact same poverty...

---

1 Tuḥaf al-'Uqūl, p. 305.

Lesson Sixty Eight
The Largest Marketplace!

Tradition:

الدُّنيا سُوقٌ رَبِحَ فِيها قَومٌ وَخَسِرَ آخَرُونَ

Imam Hādī ('a) is narrated to have said: The world is a marketplace wherein one group profits, while another group loses.[1]

Brief Commentary:

This world is not the real home of human beings; it is neither a final abode, nor is it a permanent home for us. It is in reality a grand marketplace where people invest their resources and then gain a return on what they have worked so hard for. Their resources include their intellectual, emotional, spiritual, and psychological wealth. These are the resources that we accumulate and which then lead us towards everlasting felicity and happiness in the next world.

Those who are active, hard working, and aware are cognizant of the existence of this grand marketplace and they are always busy working in order that they can 'purchase' valuable goods with the resources they have at hand. Their goal is to transform what they possess into ever more valuable goods which are everlasting; they do this for the felicity of both themselves, as well as their society. This is in contradiction to those who sell their resources for goods of ever lessening value (or in some cases, things which are of a purely corrupted and destructive nature). The end result is that those who have 'traded' well will leave this world with a load of true wealth that will last forever, while those who have 'traded' improperly will leave this world with nothing in their disposal but loss and regret.

[1] Tuḥaf al-'Uqūl, p. 361.

Lesson Sixty Nine
The Highest Ranking People

Tradition:

إنّ أعظمَ النّاسِ منزلةً عِنْدَ الله يومَ القيامَةِ أمشاهُم في أرْضِهِ بالنَّصيحَةِ لِخلْقِهِ

The Prophet (ṣ) is narrated to have said: The most eminent of the people on the Day of Judgement will be those who took the most steps in advising (seeking the best for) the creation of God.[1]

Brief Commentary:

Serving and helping the people is considered as one of the greatest acts of worship in Islam. In fact, one of the ways which one can serve God is to consider the benefit and interests of the people as one's own benefit and interest. Just as one will consider their personal interests with the utmost care and consideration, likewise one should consider the interests of the people in the same way. One should seek the best for the people both in their presence, as well as in their absence.

---

[1] Narrated from the book of Kāfī, vol. 2, p. 166.

Lesson Seventy

Three Important Social Principles

Tradition:

النَّاسُ سَواءٌ كَأَسْنانِ المِشْطِ وَالمَرءُ كَثِيرٌ بِأَخِيْهِ وَلا خَيْرَ فِي صُحْبَةِ مَنْ لَمْ يَرَ لَكَ مِثْلَ الّذي يَرى لِنَفْسِهِ

Imam Ṣādiq (ʿa) is narrated to have said: The people (in relation to their social rights) are equal to one another much like the teeth of a comb. An individual becomes many in number due to his (religious) brothers. And it is not worthy for one to sit with an individual who does not want for you what he wants for himself.[1]

Brief Commentary:

Three important principles have been mentioned in this tradition. The first is that all human beings are equal to one another in their rights, no matter their race, language, or social class. The second principle is that individuals are connected to one another in the society and the society relates back to the individual as well. In this way, an individual and his brothers are what really composes a society overall. The third principle manifests the necessity of wanting for others what one wants for himself. This is considered a primary principle of the friendship which exists among the people. A nation in which these three principles are not primary and active is neither an Islamic nation, nor a nation of true human beings.

---

[1] Tuḥaf al-ʿUqūl, p. 274.

Lesson Seventy One

To Be Hot Tempered and Rash

Tradition:

الحِدَّةُ نَوْعٌ مِنَ الجُنُونِ لأَنَّ صاحِبَها يَنْدُمُ، فَإِنْ لَمْ يَنْدُمْ فَجُنُونُه مُسْتَحْكَمٌ

Imam 'Alī ('a) is narrated to have said: Being hot tempered and rash is a type of insanity for the possessor of these attributes quickly becomes regretful over what he has done and if he does not become regretful, then his insanity has (indeed) become permanent.[1]

Brief Commentary:

Human intellect and understanding necessitates that the people should abstain from haste and rash behavior. When people act in such a manner, they are left unable to properly analyze or judge a given situation. They are soon left regretful over their hasty decision making and they realize that they clearly made a mistake. This is a mistake which most likely would not have been made if they had left aside haste and properly gauged the situation at hand.

In some cases, someone can be rash in their speech and with just a few words, they can lay waste to a lifetime of careful planning and work. With just these few words, they can lose a number of their friends whose friendship they had cultivated over many years of their lives. Such a person will be left with only regret and sorrow for their haste and their rash speech. Yet, if such an individual does not become regretful even after tasting the fruits of their haste, then such a person is truly one beset by permanent insanity.

---

[1] Nahj al-Balāghah, Aphorisms.

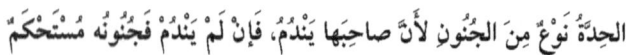

Lesson Seventy Two
The True Ascetics

Tradition:

الزُّهْدُ فِي الدُّنيا قَصْرُ الأَمَلِ وَشُكْرُ كُلِّ نِعْمَةٍ وَالوَرَعُ عَنْ كُلِّ ما حَرَّمَ اللهُ

The Prophet (ṣ) is narrated to have said: Asceticism in this world is found in three things- the cutting short of desires, thankfulness for the blessings, and abstinence from the unlawful (the Ḥarām).[1]

Brief Commentary:

A great many of the people do not have a proper understanding of asceticism in Islam and they in fact see it as a life isolated from the society and from all things related to money and wealth. Due to this idea, they see such a life as one full of hardship and something related to obscure mysticism; they see it as being contrary to progress and societal growth. This is while true asceticism is actually a progressive program of life and it can be instrumental in the building of the society at large. The narration has mentioned how true asceticism is actually found in the cutting short of desires, being thankful for one's blessings, and abstinence from what is unlawful.

[1] Tuḥaf al-'Uqūl.

Lesson Seventy Three

Examining One's Character

Tradition:

ثَلاثٌ يُمْتَحَنُ بِها عُقُولُ الرِّجالِ هُنَّ المالُ وَالوِلايَةُ وَالمُصيبَةُ

Imam 'Alī ('a) is narrated to have said: There are three things through which the intellect of great men is tested: wealth, position, and calamities.[1]

Brief Commentary:

The tests of God are a means of allowing human beings to grow and reach perfection in their day to day lives. These tests are never set in stone and they can be administered in a multitude of different ways. At the same time, there are three subject matters that are the most important when it comes to the people and these are issues related to wealth, social position, and calamities. How will a given individual react when he is given a sum of wealth; will he lose control of himself and begin to act in all sorts of outlandish ways?

How will a given person act when he is given a high ranking social position; will he again forget who he really is and become arrogant and prideful? How will someone act when he is faced with a calamity or any difficulty that he comes across in life? Will he sit in a corner and become utterly despondent, losing his sense of thankfulness towards God due to that difficulty? These are the three most important things which human beings are tested with in their lives.

---

[1] Ghurar al-Ḥikam, Root Section: Thulāth.

Lesson Seventy Four

The Correct Life Program for this World and the Next

Tradition:

اعْمَلْ لِدُنياكَ كَأَنَّكَ تَعِيشُ أَبَدًا وَاعْمَلْ لآخِرَتِكِ كأَنَّكَ تَمُوتُ غَدًا

Imam Riḍā (ʿa) is narrated to have said: Work towards the life of this world as if you will live forever and work towards the next world as if you will die tomorrow![1]

Brief Commentary:

The aforementioned tradition details how Islam views our material and spiritual lives both in this world and the next. A Muslim should be living his life in this world in such a firm and established way that it seems as if he is going to live in this world forever. This statement completely destroys the ideology of false asceticism which some people have tried to attribute to Islam.

Similarly, when it comes to spiritual issues and our preparedness for it, it is necessary to be so exact and detailed that if we were to die tomorrow, we would not have any defiencies or regrets. This means that we would have washed ourselves pure of any mistakes with true repentance and we would have paid back in full anything we owed to the people in terms of their rights and our responsibilities towards them. If we live in such a way, then it will be possible for us to die even tomorrow in a way where we are left without any regrets and sorrows over what we should have done.

---

[1] Wasā'il al-Shīʿah (according to the section Aqwāl al-Aʿimmah, vol. 2, p. 277).

Lesson Seventy Five
The Effects of Sin

Tradition:

مَنْ يَمُوتُ بِالذَّنْبِ أَكْثَرَ مِمَّنْ يَمُوتُ بِالآجالِ وَمَنْ يَعِيشُ بِالإحسانِ أَكْثَرُ مِمَّنْ يَعِيشُ بِالأَعمارِ

Imam Ṣādiq (ʻa) is narrated to have said: Those who die due to their sins are more than those who die due to their natural life spans. And those who live due to their good actions are more than those who live due to their natural life spans.[1]

Brief Commentary:

Today it has been proven that a considerable number of physical diseases have their primary roots in various spiritual problems. Similarly, one of the most important factors of psychological disease can be found in issues related to the conscience and these issues are caused by the commission of sins and the negative effects of these sins on the soul. A sinful person is in reality 'convicted' by his soul and he is likewise punished for what he has done. The effects of this punishment can be witnessed on the soul, as well as the physical body. The effects of these sins can even be seen in how and when a person dies!

Similarly, good actions have their own specific effects on the conscience and the soul. These positive actions bring about spiritual wealth and energy and they in turn have an effect on the physical body as well. They also have an effect on how long a person lives. In conclusion, it can be said that the sins shorten one's lifespan, while good actions lengthen them.

---

[1] Narrated from the book Safīnat al-Biḥār.

Lesson Seventy Six
The True Shias

Tradition:

أَبْلِغْ شِيعَتَنا أَنَّهُ لا يُنالُ ما عِنْدَ اللهِ إلّا بِعَمَلٍ

Imam Bāqir (ʿa) is narrated to have said to one of his companions: Tell our Shias (followers) that no one will reach divine blessings and mercy except through their actions.[1]

Brief Commentary:

These words of Imam Bāqir (ʿa) are an answer to those who imagine that it is enough to simply mention that one is a Shia or express affection towards the family of the Prophet (ṣ). Such people believe that one can achieve the greatest rank before God simply through such lip service, while we know that Islam is based upon action, and the true Shias are those whose program of action are based in line with the teachings of the Prophet (ṣ) and his Ahl al-Bayt (ʿa). Therefore, we should realize that the real Shia of the Prophet (ṣ) and his Ahl al-Bayt (ʿa) are those who are truly following in their footsteps, and words and expressed love alone are never enough!

---

[1] Uṣūl al-Kāfī, vol. 2, p. 300.

Lesson Seventy Seven
With Whom Should We Consult?

Tradition:

لا تَدْخِلَنَّ فِي مَشورَتِك بَخِيلًا يَعْدِلُ بِكَ عَنِ الفَضْلِ وَيَعِدُكَ الفَقْرَ
وَلا جَبانًا يُضْعِفُكَ عَنِ الأُمُورِ
وَلا حَرِيصًا يُزَيِّنُ لَكَ الشَّرَّهُ بِالجَورِ

Imam ʿAlī (ʿa) is narrated to have said: Do not consult with miserly people for they will restrain you from serving God's creation and they will make you fearful of poverty. Do not consult with cowardly people for they will weaken your will towards doing important things, and (similarly) do not consult with greedy people for they will present oppression as something (positive and) beautiful for you![1]

Brief Commentary:

To consult with others is an important concept that has been greatly encouraged in Islam. At the same time, consultation requires the initial implementation of proper planning and rules for it to be beneficial. For example, consulting with people who have clear defects in certain respects will result in receiving defective advice. Such advice will actually end up hurting you instead of helping. It is for this reason that Imam ʿAlī (ʿa) has emphasized that one should not select any of these three categories of people for advice and consultation. The emphasis on this increases as the issue being consulted upon grows in importance.

The aforementioned tradition has mentioned that the miserly, the cowardly, and the greedy are amongst those who are not to be consulted with and the reasoning is that they all im-

[1] Nahj al-Balāghah, Letter 53.

part their own particular worldview to the advice that they give. Since their worldview is deviant and misguided, their advice will similarly be misguided as well. Such people will transform generosity into miserliness, courage into cowardice, and a sense of satisfaction into greed and the willingness to oppress in order to reach one's goals.

LESSON SEVENTY EIGHT
THE BEST OF BLESSINGS

Tradition:

أَجلٌّ النِّعَمِ العافِيَةُ وَخَيْرٌ مادَامَ فِي القَلْبِ اليَقِينُ

Imam 'Alī ('a) is narrated to have said: The best blessing is health and soundness, while the best thing which can fill one's heart is faith in God.[1]

Brief Commentary:

In this tradition, Imam 'Alī ('a) has pointed out the greatest physical and spiritual blessings which one could have. Physical health is not only the greatest material blessing but it is the root of all other blessings as well. It is through means of our physical health that we are able to do everything else. Without physical health, such things like prayers, fasting, charity, and other good works would not be possible for us.

When it comes to spiritual issues, the greatest blessing that one could have is that of a heart filled with faith in God. This is something which allows us to see the world as it is and which lights the way in front of us in even the most powerful of darkness. It is through faith that the disease of ignorance and sin are eliminated and one's heart and body are made calm and peaceful.

---

[1] Tuḥaf al-'Uqūl.

Lesson Seventy Nine
The Hidden Imam (ʿa)

Tradition:

قيل للإمام جعفرٍ الصادق (عليه السلام):
كَيفَ يَنْتَفِعُ النَّاسُ بِالحُجّةِ الغائِبِ المَستُورِ؟
قَالَ: كَما يَنْتَفِعُونَ بِالشَّمسِ إذا سَتَرَها السَّحَابُ

It was asked of Imam Ṣādiq (ʿa): How do the people benefit from the existence of a hidden imam? The Imam (ʿa) answered: In the same (that one benefits) from the sun when it is behind the clouds.[1]

Brief Commentary:

The light of the sun is the driving source of all life that exists on this earth and there is no living creature that is able to continue its existence in the long term without this amazing source of energy. In this same way, the Hidden Imam (ʿa) has been likened to the power of the sun over all that exists on this earth. This doesn't only apply to their physical existence, but also their spiritual existence as well.

Even when the sun is hidden behind the clouds, it still transmits a great deal of light to the earth and this light exerts a great influence over all living things. Similarly, the Imam (ʿa) exerts a great physical and spiritual influence over the earth, even when he is hidden from the sight of the people. At the same time, it must be said that all things benefit only to the degree of their potential. In this way, the benefit of the people from the Imam (ʿa) will only be to the degree that they have developed themselves and are able to benefit from him.

---

[1] Biḥār al-Nūr, vol. 52, p. 92.

Lesson Eighty

Do Not Sit At Every Conversation

Tradition:

مَنْ أَصْغى إِلى ناطِقٍ فَقَدْ عَبَدَهُ فَإنْ كَانَ النَّاطِقُ عَنِ الله فَقَدْ عَبَدَ الله وَإِنْ كَانَ النَّاطِقُ يَنْطُقُ عَنْ لِسانِ إِبليسَ فَقَدْ عَبَدَ إِبْلِيس

Imam Jawād (ʻa) is narrated to have said: He who listens to a speaker has worshiped him. Therefore, if he speaks of God, he has worshipped God and if he speaks of Satan, he has worshipped Satan.[1]

Brief Commentary:

Whenever someone speaks in regards to any topic, he exerts a certain influence over those who hear it. Similarly, when someone listens to another's speech, he is influenced by those words as well. In this same way, words can be positive or negative, and in some cases they can be a mixture of both truth and falsehood. When one sits complacently and listens to another's speech, it is a type of worship in the sense that the words will take root in their soul and exert their own influence and effect.

So those who listen to positive and truthful words will find positivity and truth taking root in their souls, while those who listen to negative and deviant words will find that those attributes have likewise taken root in their souls. Therefore, we must always be careful not to sit in the company of negative speakers so that their words do not affect us in a negative way.

---

[1] Tuḥaf al-ʻUqūl, p. 339.

Lesson Eighty One

Those With the Attributes of Satan

Tradition:

إِذا رَأَيْتُم الرَّجُلَ لايُبالِي ما قَالَ أَو ما قِيلَ فِيْهِ فَإنَّهُ لَبَغِيَّةٌ أَو شَيطانٌ

The Prophet of Islam (ṣ) is narrated to have said: Whenever you see someone who doesn't care what he says or what people say about him, then you should know that he is either corrupt or Satanic.[1]

Brief Commentary:

When someone submerses themselves very deeply in sin, they will eventually reach the point where they don't care what they say about others or what is said in regards to them. They will give rise to the worst types of slander and they will be indifferent when the worst things are said about them. Such people are those who are worthless, corrupt, and tainted with the attributes of Satan.

[1] Biḥār al-Anwār, vol. 74, p. 147.

Lesson Eighty Two

The Real ʿĪd (Day of Celebration)

Tradition:

إنَّما هُوَ عِيدٌ لِمَنْ قَبِلَ الله صِيامَهُ وَشَكَرَ قِيامَهُ وَكُلُّ يَومٍ لا يُعْصى الله فِيْهِ فَهُوَ عِيْدٌ

Imam ʿAlī (ʿa) is narrated to have said: This day (the day of ʿĪd al-Fitr) is the ʿĪd[1] of those whose fasting and worship has been accepted by God; and every day that you do not sin is a day of ʿĪd.[2]

Brief Commentary:

The celebration that we hold after fasting for thirty days during the blessed month of Ramaḍān is in reality a celebration over our conquest of our desires and lusts. This is a celebration of our obedience to God and his commands. Therefore, such a day is a day of celebration for those who have obeyed God in his commands and have understood the ultimate philosophy of their actions. Yet for those who have dishonored such a month and who have not attempted to educate and train themselves in the obedience of God, such a day is nothing but a day of sorrow and grief.

---

[1] ʿĪd can be generally understood as a day of celebration or a holy day.

[2] Nahj al-Balāghah, Aphorism 428.

Lesson Eighty Three
Valuable Investments

Tradition:

إِنَّ اللهَ لا يَنْظُرُ إِلى صُوَرِكُم وَلا إِلى أَموَالِكُمْ وَإِنَّما يَنْظُرُ إِلى قُلُوبِكُمْ وَأَعْمَالِكُمْ

The Prophet (ṣ) is narrated to have said: God does not look at your faces and your wealth; rather, he looks at your hearts and your actions.[1]

Brief Commentary:

Even though most societies judge people based on how they look and how much money they have, Islam has explicitly mentioned that such judgements are actually incorrect and misguided. What God really judges people through are their hearts (meaning their thoughts) and their actions. Our hearts are the root of all of our actions and if we possess pure hearts, then likewise our actions will be pure and wholesome. In front of God's judgement, the only successful people are those who possess these valuable things.

[1] Muḥijat al-Bayḍā', vol. 6, p. 312.

LESSON EIGHTY FOUR
TWO THINGS WHICH CAUSE THE DESTRUCTION OF THE PEOPLE

Tradition:

أَهْلَكَ النَّاسَ إِثْنَانِ خَوْفُ الفَقْرِ وَطَلَبُ الفَخْرِ

Imam 'Alī ('a) is narrated to have said: Two things have thrown people into destruction and these are fear of poverty and the seeking of glory.[1]

Brief Commentary:

There are two things which are the root causes of the increase that we see in thievery, bribery, and various other crimes in our societies. Similarly, if we look at the root causes of greed and the insane accumulation of wealth in various individuals, we would find that such behavior is caused by this same fear of poverty and the seeking of illusory glory.

When we look at some people, we see that in spite of their possession of great amounts of wealth, they are still engaging in various illogical behaviors, such as the continuous accumulation of wealth. In some cases, they even resort to illegal actions due their root fear of becoming poverty stricken (in spite of possessing millions or even billions of dollars in wealth). In other cases, people give up that sense of calm and peace which they have in their lives, only to exchange it for the never ending seeking of glory and fame. They do this in order to compete with their rivals and to show themselves as being superior to them. This is while if they were to give up these two negative traits, their lives would be filled with ease and happiness.

---

[1] Tuḥaf al-'Uqūl.

Lesson Eighty Five
Do Not Count Such Works as Being Little!

Tradition:

لا يَقِلُّ عَمَلٌ مَعَ تَقوى وَكَيْفَ يَقِلُّ ما يُتَقَبَّلُ

Imam Sajjād (ʻa) is narrated to have said: Actions which are based on sincerity and piety are never small, even if they outwardly appear to be so. How is it possible that an action that is accepted by God could be small (in nature)?[1]

Brief Commentary:

The Quran has stated: "God only accepts the actions which are accompanied by piety and pure intentions". Therefore, we should pay close attention to the purity of our intentions, our sincerity, and our piety when it comes to our actions and not their quantity. This is because no matter how small the action may be, if it comes with sincerity and piety, then it is of great value before God and considered an action that is accepted by him. Can an action that God has accepted ever be considered as being small? In conclusion, the actions which are based on insincerity and showing off are those that are without value, and those which are based on sincerity of intention and piety are valuable and weighty in front of God.

[1] Tuḥaf al-ʻUqūl, p. 201.

Lesson Eighty Six
Do Not Make Mistakes So That You Don't Have to Apologize

Tradition:

إِيَّاكَ وَما تَعْتَذِرُ مِنْهُ فَإِنَّ الْمُؤمِنَ لا يَسِيىءُ وَلا يَعْتَذِرُ وَالْمُنافِقُ كُلَّ يَوْمٍ يَسِيىءُ وَيَعْتَذِرُ

Imam Ḥusayn ('a) is narrated to have said: Do not perform bad actions for then apologizing will be an inevitable consequence. This is because a believing person performs neither bad actions, nor does he apologize (as a consequence of the bad actions). Yet the hypocrite performs bad actions and seeks pardon every day.[1]

Brief Commentary:

It is possible for every individual to make a mistake but the people of faith and the hypocrites have a critical difference in this regard. This difference is that the believers strive to make less mistakes so that they won't have to keep making amends for them because they realize that apologizing is only a second best after one has already done something wrong. One of the marks of the believers is someone who quickly learns and does not keep making mistakes; this is also in line with the issue of faith where one's inner reality is the same as their outer reality. Therefore, if they are pure internally, then this will reflect clearly on their behavior as well.

[1] Taken from the book Tuḥaf al-'Uqūl, p. 177.

Lesson Eighty Seven
The Worst Way of Living

Tradition:

أَسْوَءَ النَّاسِ مَعاشًا ... مَنْ لَمْ يَعِشْ غَيْرُهُ فِي مَعاشِهِ

Imam Riḍā ('a) is narrated to have said: The worst of the people in respect to their economic lives are those who do not support others with their livelihood...[1]

Brief Commentary:

A healthy economy is one where social bonds are made strong and connect all of the people to one another. A society where various classes are created towards the benefit of the few is a society that is rotten and sick to the core. Imam Riḍā ('a) has mentioned in this tradition that the life in which others are not supported is the worst kind of economic life possible.

[1] Taken from the book Tuḥaf al-'Uqūl, p. 334.

Lesson Eighty Eight
Our Promises Are Our Debts

Tradition:

إنّا أَهْلُ بَيتٍ نَرى وَعْدَنا عَلَينا دَيْنًا كَما صَنَعَ رَسُولُ الله صلّى الله عليه وآله

Imam Riḍā ('a) is narrated to have said: We are a family who consider our promises to be just like our debts (and) this is how the Prophet of God (ṣ) was.[1]

Brief Commentary:

Debts are not related only to when we borrow something from others and then owe them money as a result. Those who give their word and promise to others are in reality in their debt and they are responsible to fulfill their moral and ethical obligation towards them. This is something which they can't simply shrug off!

Being loyal to one's word is a sign of character, faith, truthfulness, and it also helps to solidify the bonds of trust in the society. It is something which enlivens the spirit of social cooperation and it is for these reasons that Islam has placed a great importance on fulfilling one's promises.

[1] Taken from the book Tuḥaf al-'Uqūl, p. 333.

LESSON EIGHTY NINE
THE PROPERTY OF THE PEOPLE

Tradition:

إنَّ الرَّجُلَ إِذا أصابَ مالًا مِنْ حَرامٍ لَمْ يُقْبَلْ مِنْهُ حَجٌّ ولا عُمْرَةٌ ولا صِلَةُ رَحِمٍ

Imam Bāqir ('a) is narrated to have said: Whenever an individual takes in wealth through unlawful means, neither his Ḥajj and 'Umrah pilgrimage, nor his acts to strengthen his family relationships will be accepted (from him).[1]

Brief Commentary:

Good intentions by themselves are not enough in Islam. What is further necessary is the purity of the means through which we perform these good actions as well. Those who perform good actions though illegitimate means will never reach their end goal in the way that they seek. Until the means are as pure as the intentions behind them, neither of them will be accepted before God!

[1] Safīnat al-Biḥār, vol. 1, p. 213.

Lesson Ninety
Do Not Seek Things from the People As Much As Possible

Tradition:

طَلَبُ الحَوائِجِ إلَى النَّاسِ مَذلَّةٌ لِلحَياةِ ومُذْهِبَةٌ لِلحَياءِ وَاسْتِخفَافٌ بِالوِقارِ وَهُوَ الفَقْرُ الحاضِرُ

Imam Sajjād (ʻa) is narrated to have said: Requesting things from the people is (a kind) of abjectness in life and it destroys one's humility and weakens one's character and standing. It is a (type of) poverty that the people prepare for themselves.[1]

Brief Commentary:

Some people throw themselves into poverty due to actions which they believe will actually save them from it. They request things from the people which are not necessary for them and they make themselves dependent and needy upon them. Through such behavior, their character is weakened and ruined in front of others. Islam has ordered its adherents to stand upon their own two feet as much as possible and to be wary of dependence in their lives. This is because taking care of one's needs through others is the worst type of neediness and poverty!

---

[1] Taken from the book Tuḥaf al-ʻUqūl, p. 201.

Lesson Ninety One
Woe Upon Such a Person!

Tradition:

يا سَوأَتاهُ لِمَنْ غَلَبَتْ أَحْداتُهُ عَلَى عَشَرَاتِهِ

Imam Sajjād (ʿa) is narrated to have said: Woe upon he whose ones exceed his tens![1]

Brief Commentary:

The Quran has mentioned that: "Whoever brings virtue shall receive ten times its like; but whoever brings vice shall not be requited except with its like..."[2] This tradition is mentioning that the truly wretched are those whose tens (their good deeds which are rewarded ten times as much as what they have performed) are exceeded by their bad deeds (for which they are only punished once to the degree of what they have done). Imagine that God is rewarding you ten times for the good you have done and only punishing you to the degree of the sins but in spite of this the good is still outweighed by the bad! This is truly the ultimate disgrace and wretchedness.

[1] Taken from the book Tuḥaf al-ʿUqūl, p. 203.
[2] Surah Anʿām, Verse 161.

Lesson Ninety Two

Do Not Attempt To Resolve Your Problems through the Commission of Sins

Tradition:

مَنْ حاوَلَ أمراً بِمَعْصِيَةِ الله كَانَ أفْوَتُ لِما يَرجُو وأَسْرَعُ لِما يَحْذَرُ

Imam Ḥusayn (ʿa) is narrated to have said: He who seeks to do something through sinning against God will lose what he hopes for sooner and he will reach what he feared for more quickly.[1]

Brief Commentary:

Some people imagine that they will reach their goals sooner if they resort to unlawful (Ḥarām) means. For example, someone may be in a financial bind and they may think that by opening up a liquor store, they can save themselves from their financial problems and gain lots of profit from it. This is while the aforementioned tradition has explicitly mentioned that this is not the case and in fact, they will become even further engulfed in various issues than before.

In other cases, some people may think that because they are constantly suffering from financial issues, once they make more money they can finally gain a sense of inner peace and calm. They then imagine that the quickest way to make this money will be through various unlawful means. Once they have made this money, they realize that they haven't gained any additional peace in their lives and in fact, they have lost what they previously possessed as well. In addition, they may have even gained more worry and anxiety than before. This shows that we should never seek what we want and need through unlawful means; such actions will only take us further and further from our goals.

---

[1] Taken from the book Tuḥaf al-ʿUqūl, p. 977.

Lesson Ninety Three

Those Who Are Satisfied With Themselves!

Tradition:

مَنْ رَضِيَ عَنْ نَفْسِهِ كَثُرَ السَّاخِطُ عَلَيهِ

Imam ʿAlī (ʿa) is narrated to have said: He who is self satisfied and egotistic will have many who are not happy with him.[1]

Brief Commentary:

Although confidence and having love for oneself at a moderate level is necessary for the continuation of life, it can exceed these normal boundaries and reach a point of selfishness and egoism. Those who are egotistical never see their own personal faults and they consider themselves to be pure, without any fault, and loveable all at the same time. They believe they are the cream of the crop in their society and the best at everything that they do. For this same reason, they have great expectations from the people and this causes the people to resent and eventually hate them.

[1] Nahj al-Balāghah, Aphorism 6.

Lesson Ninety Four
Close and Far Relatives

Tradition:

القَرِيبُ مَنْ قَرَّبَتْهُ المَوَدَّةُ وَإِنْ بَعُدَ نَسَبُهُ وَالبَعِيدُ مَنْ باعَدَتْهُ المَوَدَّةُ وَإِنْ قَرُبَ نَسَبُهُ

Imam Ḥasan al-Mujtabā ('a) is narrated to have said: One's close relatives are those who have the most love for you, even if they are far in relation to lineage. And the far relatives are those who have less love and affection for you, even if they are from your close relatives.[1]

Brief Commentary:

The relationship between relatives is one of the most important social institutions in Islam. Such relationships are comprised of tighter knit groups in the society where cooperation can extend to a higher and greater degree than in the society overall. This relationship is instrumental in the resolution of problems that come up from time to time. This tradition has emphasized that these relationships must in reality be based on love and affection and not only on simple lineage and family blood!

[1] Taken from the book Tuḥaf al-'Uqūl, p. 165.

Lesson Ninety Five
Breaking Bad Habits

Tradition:

رَدُّ المُعْتادِ عَنْ عادَتِهِ كَالمُعْجِزِ

Imam Ḥasan ʿAskarī (ʿa) is narrated to have said: Breaking the incorrect habits of the people is much like a miracle![1]

Brief Commentary:

Habits are actually one of the great divine blessings because it makes difficult things easy to do for people. Many of the complex and difficult tasks which we must do in our day to day lives (such as speaking, walking, etc...) are made automatic through their habitual nature. At the same time, habits can also establish incorrect actions and make them automatic in nature as well. When negative behavior becomes enshrined in habit, it becomes very dangerous and eliminating it from our lives is transformed into a very difficult task. Imam ʿAskarī (ʿa) has considered the breaking of such habits to be similar in nature to a miracle. Therefore, we should strive our utmost not to cultivate negative habits to begin with and this will make it unnecessary for us to spend great amounts of time attempting to break them later on in our lives.

[1] Biḥār al-Anwār, vol. 17, p. 217.

LESSON NINETY SIX
THE TRAGEDY OF KARBALĀ

Tradition:

لا وَاللهِ لا أُعْطِيهِم بِيَدِي إِعْطاءَ الذَّلِيلِ وَلا أَفِرُّ فِرارَ الْعَبِيدِ... ، إِنِّي لا أَرى الْمَوتَ إلّا سَعادَةً، وَالحَياةَ مَعَ الظّالِمِينَ إلّا بَرَمًا

Imam Ḥusayn (ʿa) is narrated to have said: I swear by God that I will never put my hand in theirs[1] like an abject person nor will I run away like the slaves... I see death as nothing but felicity and life with the oppressors as nothing but the cause of misery and affliction![2]

Brief Commentary:

The day of ʿĀshūrā' is a day that will never be forgotten and it can be considered as a great university for all of mankind. It is a great university for all people who wish to live and die with honor and greatness. The lessons that were taught on that day can fill volumes with its wisdom. The aforementioned lines from Imam Ḥusayn (ʿa) are but a small indication of who he was and how he lived his life. If we study his life and the lessons of that momentous day, surely we too will be able to live and die with full honor and greatness as well.

---

[1] In order to pledge allegiance to Yazīd.
[2] Maqtal al-Ḥusayn, pgs. 246 and 256.

Lesson Ninety Seven

Who is the Intelligent One?

Tradition:

العاقِلُ هُوَ الّذي يَضَعُ الشَّيءَ مَوَاضِعَهُ

Imam 'Alī ('a) was requested to describe the signs of someone who is intelligent. He replied by saying: The intelligent one is he who places everything in its proper place.[1]

Brief Commentary:

There is much that has been said in regards to what intelligence actually is; out of all of what has been said, the short tradition above is the best description of what intelligence truly is. Intelligence is nothing but the placement of all things in their proper place. Such an individual will position every person in the society in their own proper place. Similarly, happiness and sorrow, friendship and enmity, mildness and harshness, affection, worship, work, leisure, and all other things will be positioned in their proper place. When all of these things are thus positioned, then that individual is truly one who is the epitome of intelligence.

[1] Nahj al-Balāghah, Aphorisms.

Lesson Ninety Eight
The Cause of Enmity

Tradition:

النَّاسُ أَعْدَاءُ ما جَهِلُوا

Imam ʿAlī (ʿa) is narrated to have said: The people are enemies of what they do not know.[1]

Brief Commentary:

We see that some people reject a great many things which are real and they stand up against them in opposition. Their only reason for such things is they don't understand them or it is something new to them. This wise saying is particularly true in regards to religious matters. Some people easily reject religious matters when they don't understand them and this applies even to those who are learned in another field.

You would think that someone who has taken the time to learn another field would understand that it takes much work in order to master a given field and therefore they should not be so quick to judge something which they don't understand. When we pay attention to these religious matters, we realize how deep they really are. Therefore, we should be careful never to reject something simply because it may seem strange to us or because we don't understand it.

[1] Nahj al-Balāghah, Aphorisms, sentence 172.

LESSON NINETY NINE
THE ONES WHO POSSESSES GHAYRAH[1]

Tradition:

إنّ الله تَعالى يُحِبُّ مِنْ عِبادِهِ الغَيُورَ

The Prophet (ṣ) is narrated to have said: God the Almighty loves those of his servants who are Ghayūr.[2]

Brief Commentary:

Ghayrah is in reality a sense of loyalty and a sense of protectiveness over one's religion or family. It can even extend to wanting to protect the Islamic lands as well. A Ghayūr individual feels responsible towards protecting these things and becomes extremely upset when a stranger encroaches upon them. Ghayrah is one of the prominent characteristics of the prophets and the men of God. It has been mentioned that Prophet Abraham ('a) possessed this characteristic and so in conclusion this is a powerful characteristic and force that is critical against attacks by outsiders against our religion, our families, and our people.

---

[1] This term refers to those who have a protective sense towards their religion, their people, or their family. An individual who possesses this feeling of wishing to protect these things is called Ghayūr, which refers to one who has Ghayrah).

[2] Nahj al-Faṣāḥah, p. 15.

Lesson One Hundred
A Blessed Existence

Tradition:

مَثَلُ المُؤمِنِ مَثَلُ النَّخْلَةِ ما أَخَذْتَ مِنْها مِنْ شَيءٍ نَفَعَكَ

The Prophet (ṣ) is narrated to have said: The believing individual is much like a date tree. Everything that comes from it is beneficial and advantageous.[1]

Brief Commentary:

The date palm is a tree that is full of advantageous uses and blessings. We are able to eat from its fruit, which is considered as one of the healthiest and most nutritious fruits that exists. Its seeds can be used as fuel for a fire and its palm fronds can be woven into mats, hats, and table covers. Its wood can be used in buildings, as well as in the construction of bridges which pass over rivers. Its blossoms can also be used in fragrant perfumes and so every single part of this palm has a use and the tree in its entirety is of great blessing for the people.

People who have faith are similar to this tree when it comes to their benefits. Their thoughts, their words, their gatherings, their friendship, their decision making, and in reality everything which comes from them is blessed and helps the people. Their every facet is full of advantage and blessing for their societies!

---

[1] Nahj al-Faṣāḥah, p. 564.

Lesson One Hundred and One
The Best of Hands

Tradition:

الأَيدِي ثَلاثَةٌ: سائِلَةٌ وَمُمْسِكَةٌ وَمُنْفِقَةٌ وَخَيْرُ الأَيدِي المُنْفِقَةُ

The Prophet (ṣ) is narrated to have said: There are three kinds of hands- the hand which takes, the hand which remains, and the hand which gives. And the best of hands are the hands that give![1]

Brief Commentary:

Islam has always encouraged its followers to do their best and work hard in life. This has extended not only to the physical and material, but the spiritual and emotional as well. In addition, it has taught them to be independent as much as possible and not seek things from other people when they can simply work and earn it themselves. Not only has the religion asked that they not seek things from others but it has recommended that they put themselves in a position where they are the ones who are giving back. This tradition is establishing this same concept that the best of hands are those that are giving to others, and not those that are simply taking!

[1] Tuḥaf al-'Uqūl, p. 32.

Lesson One Hundred and Two

Worse Than Death

Tradition:

خَيْرٌ مِنَ الحَياةِ ما إذا فَقَدْتَهُ أَبْغَضْتَ الحَياةَ وَشَرٌّ مِنَ المَوْتِ ما إذا نَزَلَ بِكَ أَحْبَبْتَ المَوتَ

Imam Ḥasan ʿAskarī (ʿa) is narrated to have said: What is better than life is that which if you lose, you will become fed up with life. And what is worse than death is that which if you gain, you will welcome death with open arms![1]

Brief Commentary:

Some people imagine that the most valuable thing in life is found in those things which relate to the material and this is while there are a multitude of things much greater in value. People come across moments in their lives when they only wish for death and there are also some realities for which someone would be willing to sacrifice themselves in an instant for the fulfillment of those values.The martyrs who die in the way of God are those who have fully understood these words of Imam ʿAskarī (ʿa). These are people who see death as a doorway to a vaster world that is filled with felicity and the satisfaction of their Lord; they say their goodbyes to this material world and hasten to a world that is ever lasting and perfect.

---

[1] Taken from the book Tuḥaf al-ʿUqūl, p. 368.

LESSON ONE HUNDRED AND THREE

THE DIFFERENCE BETWEEN A BELIEVER AND A HYPOCRITE

Tradition:

إِذَا رَأَيْتُمُ الْمُؤْمِنَ صَمُوتًا فَادْنُوا مِنْهُ فَإِنَّهُ يُلْقِي الْحِكْمَةَ وَالْمُؤْمِنُ قَلِيلُ الْكَلَامِ

كَثِيرُ الْعَمَلِ وَالْمُنَافِقُ كَثِيرُ الْكَلَامِ قَلِيلُ الْعَمَلِ

The Prophet (ṣ) is narrated to have said: Whenever you see a believing individual engrossed in silence, then gather close to him for you will hear words full of wisdom from him. Faithful individuals are of few words and much action, while the hypocrites are of many words and few actions![1]

Brief Commentary:

Human beings are not unlimited in their power and energy and it is for this reason that when they expend much of their energy towards a specific task, they will find themselves limited in what they can do in regards to another. Therefore, it is not surprising that people who speak too much will fall short when it comes to their actions.

The Prophet of Islam (ṣ), who was a supporter of everything that was positive and helped the people, has described the people of faith as those who are filled with the spirit of hard work, rather than the spirit of talkativeness. The hypocrites, who are devoid of the spirit of faith, are the opposite to this and they spend their time talking instead of working. We should always strive to be like those the Prophet (ṣ) has described as believers and not those who are hypocrites.

---

[1] Taken from the book Tuḥaf al-'Uqūl, p. 296.

Lesson One Hundred and Four
The Best Inheritance

Tradition:

خَيْرُ ما وَرَّثَ الآباءَ الأَبناءَ الأَدَبُ

Imam 'Alī ('a) is narrated to have said: The best thing which parents leave behind for their children is good behavior.[1]

Brief Commentary:

Good behavior is defined by the positive way that we interact with others and the respect and generosity of spirit that we show to them. In some cases, good behavior is exhibited in front of God's creation, while in other cases, it is exhibited in front of God himself. In both cases, it is one of the greatest resources which human beings possess and it is the key to their success in all aspects of life.

For this same reason, Imam 'Alī ('a) has considered the greatest inheritance which parents can leave for their children as good behavior which they teach to them. Good behavior is the root of love, ease in living, friendship, and even unity. It is an important factor in how effective our speech is and how well we are able to progress in our social lives.

[1] Ghurar al-Ḥikam, p. 393.

Lesson One Hundred and Five
Respecting Freedom of Thought

Tradition:

بِئسَ القَومُ قَومٌ يَمْشِي المُؤمِنُ فِيهِمْ بالتَّقِيَّةِ وَالكِتْمانِ

The Prophet (ṣ) is narrated to have said: When a believing individual is forced to hide his beliefs and live in a hidden manner amongst a group of people, they are truly a bad people![1]

Brief Commentary:

When one is forced to hide their true beliefs and is not able to speak or practice them freely, then this is a sign that a selfish majority has forced their views on others and they are preventing the minority from expressing their thoughts and beliefs. There is no doubt that such a society will never be able to reach felicity.

Righteous people who live in a proper and healthy society must always be given the right to practice their beliefs and to express their thoughts as they wish. If they comprise a minority in that society, the majority should never prevent them from living in this manner. Their rights should be respected and they should be left free to propagate the truth.

[1] Nahj al-Faṣāḥah.

Lesson One Hundred and Six
Six Characteristics Which Are Not Present in the Believers

Tradition:

سِتَّةٌ لا تَكُونُ فِي مُؤمِنٍ: العُسْرُ وَالنَّكْدُ وَالحَسَدُ وَاللَّجاجَةُ وَالكِذْبُ وَالبَغيُ

Imam Ṣādiq ('a) is narrated to have said: There are six things which do not exist in the believing individuals- severity, ill manners, jealousy, stubbornness, lying, and oppression.[1]

Brief Commentary:

Those who have only taken the title of believers are fooling themselves if they possess certain attributes and characteristics. At the very least, the true believers must be clear of the six negative attributes mentioned in this tradition. What is interesting is that these six characteristics are all connected to how people relate to one another socially. The true believers are those who are easy going, good natured, benevolent, and submit to the truth. They are furthermore truthful, just, and justice seeking for others. The title of a believer is an extremely high ranking title that is unsuitable for those who possess the aforementioned six attributes. We should judge ourselves first and foremost and see if we possess any of these six attributes!

---

[1] Taken from Tuḥaf al-'Uqūl, p. 282.

Lesson One Hundred and Seven
Do Not Cut Off All of Your Connections

Tradition:

اتّقِ الله بَعْضَ التُّقى وَإِنْ قَلَّ وَدَعْ بَيْنَكَ وَبَيْنَهُ سِتْراً وَإِنْ رَقَ

Imam Ṣādiq ('a) is narrated to have said: Be careful of (your duty to) God and sanctify him even if only a little. Place a curtain between him and yourself even if it is very thin.[1]

Brief Commentary:

When some people begin to walk on the path of sin, they begin to walk so quickly that they cut off all of their previous connections with God. They burn all of their bridges and they seal shut all of the doors which would make their return possible. In this tradition, Imam Ṣādiq ('a) is saying that such people should at least not burn their final bridge and they should leave some sort of a way for their return. One day, such individuals will naturally feel regret for what has taken place and they should have some path ready and available for their return.

[1] Taken from Tuḥaf al-'Uqūl, p. 268.

Lesson One Hundred and Eight
The True Worship

Tradition:

يا كُمَيلُ لَيسَ الشَّأنُ أَنْ تُصَلِّي وتَصُومَ وتَتَصدَّقَ، الشَّأنُ أَنْ تَكُونَ الصَّلاةُ بِقَلبٍ نَقِيٍّ وَعَمَلٍ عِنْدَ اللهِ مَرضِيٍّ وَخُشُوعٍ سَوِيٍ

Imam 'Alī ('a) is narrated to have said to Kumayl: Oh Kumayl, it is not important that you simply pray, fast, and give in the way of God. What is important is that you pray (and perform the rest of your actions) with a heart that is pure and in a way that is worthy of God and that (your acts) are infused with humility.[1]

Brief Commentary:

The real value of our actions is not based on how many times we do them, but the quality that they are done with. It is the inner reality of worship that is important and not just its outer manifestations. In this tradition, Imam 'Alī ('a) emphasizes to Kumayl that simply sufficing with the outer aspects of worship and their quantity is not enough. It is necessary for one to go to the heart of the matter. It is this inner reality which helps us to grow and reach human completion. We should always keep this point in mind and attempt to perform our acts of worship with the purest of intentions and with the utmost levels of care.

[1] Taken from Tuḥaf al-'Uqūl, p. 117.

Lesson One Hundred and Nine
Do Not Forget Your Defects!

Tradition:

إِذا رَأَيتُمْ العَبْدَ يَتَفَقَّدُ الذُنُوبَ مِنَ النَّاسِ ناسِيًا لِذَنْبِهِ فَاعْلَمُوا أَنَّهُ قَدْ مُكِرَ بِهِ

Imam Ṣādiq (ʻa) is narrated to have said: Know that when someone is seeking out the sins of the people and criticizing them, but he has at the same time forgotten his own sins, that he has been entangled in divine punishment.[1]

Brief Commentary:

There are many people who are quite brazen in criticizing others and finding out their faults, but at the same time, they are completely unaware of their own negative points. They may criticize others for their small faults while they ignore their own major problems. Such people have been afflicted with selfishness and egoism due to the veils of arrogance and unawareness, which have covered their eyes from seeing the reality. The superior individual is the one who first removes his own defects before even looking at the defects of others.

---

[1] Taken from Tuḥaf al-ʻUqūl, p. 271.

Lesson One Hundred and Ten
The Great Torture

Tradition:

مَنْ ساءَ خُلُقُهُ عَذَّبَ نَفْسَهُ

Imam Ṣādiq ('a) is narrated to have said: He who is ill mannered torments himself.[1]

Brief Commentary:

It is commonly understood that those people who have a bad attitude and are always ill mannered towards others are a cause of their friends and close relatives' torment. By associating with such a person, they undergo various hardships and difficulties due to their negative behavior. While this is no doubt correct, such people are actually a source of the greatest torment for themselves and their entire lives are made bitter and unlivable as a result. Such negative and pessimistic people usually live shorter lives, they spend their days upset at everything, and they see all thing in a negative light.

Opposite to this is someone who has good behavior and who sees life in a positive light. This type of demeanor and viewpoint is actually considered a type of great worship by the religion of Islam and it has been greatly emphasized and encouraged. It is counted as one of the important factors which allows us to gain entry to paradise.

---

[1] Taken from Tuḥaf al-'Uqūl, p. 270.

LESSON ONE HUNDRED AND ELEVEN
THE VITALITY AND FRESHNESS OF
THE QURAN

Tradition:

إِنَّ اللهَ لَمْ يَجْعَلْ الْقُرآنَ لِزَمَانٍ دُونَ زَمَانٍ، وَلِنَاسٍ دُونَ نَاسٍ، فَهُوَ لِكُلِّ زَمَانٍ جَدِيدٌ، وَعِنْدَ كُلِّ قَوْمٍ غَضٌّ إِلَى يَوْمِ القِيَامَةِ

Imam Riḍā ('a) is narrated to have said: God has not made the Quran for a specific time period, nor for a specific group of people. Therefore, during every time period, it is new and fresh for every group.[1]

Brief Commentary:

The Imam ('a) mentioned these words when someone asked him why the Quran never gets old, even after countless recitations. The Imam ('a) pointed out this reality for him that the Quran was not created of this world, which is oft changing and in constant flux. This was a book which is rooted in God's lofty knowledge and so it is of an eternal nature. When something is of an eternal nature, then whatever comes from it will always be fresh and captivating. Indeed, this is one of the signs of the greatness and high rank of the Quran.

---

[1] Safīnat al-Biḥār, vol. 2, p. 413.

Lesson One Hundred and Twelve
Be Fearful of Worshipping Your passions

Tradition:

احْذَرُوا أَهوَائَكُم كَما تَحْذَرُونَ أَعْدَائَكُمْ فَلَيسَ شَيءٌ أَعْدى لِلرِّجالِ مِنْ اتِّباعِ أَهوَائِهِمْ وَحَصائِدِ أَلسِنَتِهِم

Imam Ṣādiq (ʻa) is narrated to have said: Fear your passions and desires just as you fear your (vehement) enemies, for the people have no worse enemy than following their passions and the end result of the words that they speak![1]

Brief Commentary:

There is no doubt that internal enemies are more dangerous than external enemies. It is for this same reason that our rebellious passions and desires, which influence us from the darkest recesses of our hearts, are more dangerous than any other enemy we can possibly face. The worship of these dark desires blind the eyes and seal the ears of the people; they shut down the proper functioning of the intellect and make us unable to see the true realities. As a result, such a person is thrown into the depths of deviation and corruption.

---

[1] Safīnat al-Biḥār, vol. 2, root word Hawā.

Lesson One Hundred and Thirteen

The Only Way to Be a Shia!

Tradition:

بَلِّغْ شِيْعَتِي عَنِّي السَّلامُ وَأَعْلِمْهُمْ أَنَّهُ لا قَرَابَةَ بَيْنَنا وَبَيْنَ اللهِ عَزَّ وَجَلَّ وَلا يُتَقَرَّبُ إِلَيهِ إِلّا بِالطّاعَةِ لَهُ

Imam Bāqir (ʻa) is narrated to have said to Jābir ibn Juʻfī: Send my greetings to my Shias and tell them that there is no link between us and God but rather the only way to gain nearness to God is through obeying his commands.[1][2]

Brief Commentary:

There are many people who think that by just being of the Shias or having love towards the family the prophet (ʻa), that this will somehow save them in and of itself. They believe that by simply stating that they love the Ahl al-Bayt, they will be counted as amongst their followers. They furthermore think that since the Imams and the Ahl al-Bayt are close to God, they will then use their influence to save them. This is while the only relationship between God and his creation is that based on following and obeying his commands. Whoever obeys God's commands the most will be closest to him and whoever commits sins will be further from him, whoever he may be!

---

[1] This tradition is referring to the fact that the Imams (ʻa) do not have a special link with God whereby they are simply given a position near to God due to that link. Our relationship with God is based on obeying his commands and not by dint of anything else.

[2] Biḥār al-Anwār, vol. 15, p. 164.

Lesson One Hundred and Four-teen

The Relationship between Wealth and its Consumption

Tradition:

مَنْ يَكْسِبُ مالًا مِنْ غَيْرِ حَقِّهِ يَصْرِفُهُ فِي غَيْرِ أَجْرِهِ

Imam ʿAlī (ʿa) is narrated to have said: He who gains wealth through unlawful means will spend that wealth in a way which will entail no divine reward.[1]

Brief Commentary:

People oftentimes say that that not just any money is worthy of being spent in positive ways and the money must first be gained in pure and lawful ways. This tradition shows the veracity of this common saying. How can people think that if the money they have has been gained in unlawful ways, they will somehow be able to gain positive results for themselves by spending it in good ways? How can any reward be expected when the source of that money was unlawful to begin with?

Such money may even end up having consequences that are completely opposite to what was originally intended. On the other hand, even a small amount of money which is gained in lawful ways, may end up having tremendously positive effects. Therefore, we should always keep in mind that the root of money and the way through which it is earned have an effect both on the end result, as well as the reward which is given for such good actions.

[1] Taken from the book Tuḥaf al-ʿUqūl, p. 63

Lesson One Hundred and Fifteen
The Most Truthful and the Most Learned

Tradition:

لِكُلِّ أُمَّةٍ صِدِّيقٌ وَفارُوقٌ، وَصِدِّيقُ هٰذه الأمّة وَفارُوقُها عَلَيٌّ بنُ أَبي طالِبٍ
عليه السلام

The Prophet (ṣ) is narrated to have said: Every nation has its Ṣiddīq and Farūq,[1] and the Ṣiddīq and Farūq of this nation is ʿAlī ibn Abī Ṭālib.[2]

Brief Commentary:

In order to implement and organize a proper and cohesive religious society, it was necessary for there to be someone capable who could lead after the passing of the Prophet of Islam (ṣ). The Prophet (ṣ) had spent many of his years engaged in building the very basic foundations of the Islamic society. Much time had also been spent fighting against the polytheists and other enemies of the new faith.

Someone was necessary to continue this building process and to separate and distinguish between the truth and the falsehood (in essence, someone who was a Farūq). Someone was also necessary in order to explain the realities of Islam openly and clearly (who would be known as a Ṣiddīq) in order that all the questions of the people be properly answered. Such a person could only be ʿAlī ibn Abī Ṭālib and no one else in the society was capable of fulfilling such a position.

---

[1] The term Ṣiddīq can be understood to mean a truthful individual and the term Farūq can be understood as one who discerns and distinguishes between the truth and the falsehood.

[2] Safīnat al-Biḥār, vol. 2, p. 221.

Lesson One Hundred and Sixteen

Simple Living and Cooperation in the Management of Home Life

Tradition:

كَانَ عَلِيٌّ (عليه السلام) يَحْتَطِبُ وَيَسْتَقِي وَيَكْنُسُ وَكَانَتْ فَاطِمَةُ تَطْحَنُ وَتَعْجِنُ وَتَخْبِزُ

Imam Ṣādiq (ʻa) is narrated to have said: ʻAlī (ʻa) would bring firewood from the desert (for use in the home), he would bring water, and he would clean, while Fāṭimah (ʻa) would make flour, turn it into dough, and bake bread.[1]

Brief Commentary:

This tradition is a small window into the lives of Imam ʻAlī (ʻa) and the Lady Fāṭimah (ʻa) and how they would conduct their day to day affairs. They lived their lives with the utmost simplicity and without any excess or waste. Their lives were filled with happiness, affection, cooperation, and vitality. Work was not seen as something to be shied away from, while cooperation and understanding were seen as a foundation of life. Unfortunately, these are things which have been lost in modern day life and along with them, we have also lost much of our day to day peace and tranquility.

[1] Safīnat al-Biḥār, vol. 2, p. 195.

Lesson One Hundred and Seventeen
One Hour of Justice

Tradition:

عَدْلُ ساعَةٍ خَيْرٌ مِنْ عِبادَةِ سَنَةٍ

The Prophet (ṣ) is narrated to have said: One hour of (the implementation of) justice is better than a year of worship.[1]

Brief Commentary:

Worship is the connection between the creator and the created and understanding this relationship holds many inner lessons for us and it brings about the growth and progression of the intellect and the spirit of human beings. In spite of this importance that worship holds, the tradition above surprisingly says that one hour where justice is implemented is superior to one year of extra worship. The question comes up as to how such a thing can be possible? In other traditions, we also see mentioned how one hour of contemplation and thought are superior to one whole night (or according to other traditions, one whole year's worship). What this tradition is showing us is how important justice (as well as thinking and contemplation) are in God's eyes. What is interesting to note is that both contemplation and justice have common roots, since where there is no justice, there can also be no thought or contemplation!

---

[1] Nahj al-Faṣāḥah, p. 410.

Lesson One Hundred and Eighteen
The True Doctor

Tradition:

الطَّبِيبُ الله وَلَعَلَّكَ تَرْفَقُ بِأَشياءَ تَخْرِقُ بِها غَيْرَكَ

The Prophet (ṣ) is narrated to have said: The true physician is God and it is possible that there are some things which are beneficial for you that others see as being harmful.[1]

Brief Commentary:

In some cases, many of the difficulties that people face in their lives are caused by a lack of proper thinking or a lack of proper choice. In some other cases, people are faced with certain undesirable events which are not caused by their own choices and they become needful of a 'physician' which can cure them. This master physician is none other than Allah, who possesses powerful types of medicine which can completely cure his ill patients. In some cases, these medicines can be quite bitter and difficult to take but they have powerful and beneficial effects on the diseases which the people face. In all cases, God is the master physician, and even though his medicine may initially seem difficult to take, he is the most aware of how best to cure his ill patients.

[1] Nahj al-Faṣāḥah, p. 406.

Lesson One Hundred and Nineteen
The Successors of the Prophets

Tradition:

لا يَزالُ هٰذا الدِّينُ عَزِيزاً مَنِيعًا إِلى اثْنَي عَشَرَ كُلُّهُمْ مِنْ قُرَيشٍ

The Prophet (ṣ) is narrated to have said: This religion will always be eminent and safe from the hands of the enemies until twelve individuals have ruled and all of them will be from the Quraysh.[1]

Brief Commentary:

Many of the most accepted books of the Ahl al-Sunnah have mentioned similar traditions in regards to the twelve leaders. These books include: Ṣaḥīḥ Bukhārī, Ṣaḥīḥ Muslim, Ṣaḥīḥ Tirmidhī, Ṣaḥīḥ Abū Dawūd, Masnad Aḥmad, as well as many others. These narrations number around 271 when we count all of the Shia and Sunni sources through which they have been narrated. What is even more interesting is that these twelve rulers cannot correspond to anything other than the twelve Shia Imams when we look at the entirety of Islamic history.

When we look at the first three caliphs or the caliphs of the Ummayads and the Abbasids, none of them can be found to be amongst these twelve who have been mentioned. Due to this reason, the scholars of the Ahl al-Sunnah have met with a great difficulty in trying to decipher and categorize who these twelve actually are. Yet, at the same time, the Shias have easily understood who these traditions are referring to and have clearly identified these twelve rulers.

---

[1] Taken from the book Taysīr al-Wuṣūl, written by Zubaydī Shāfiʿī.

Lesson One Hundred and Twenty
A Gathering of Sin

Tradition:

لا يَنْبَغِي لِلمُؤمِنِ أنْ يَجْلِسَ مَجْلِسًا يُعْصى اللهُ فِيْهِ وَلا يَقْدِرُ عَلَىٰ تَغْيِيرِهِ

Imam Ṣādiq ('a) is narrated to have said: It is not worthy of the believers to sit in a gathering where there is sin while they are unable to stop it.[1]

Brief Commentary:

Participating in a gathering of sin is a sin itself even if the individual does not commit any sin and he doesn't become like the people of that gathering. This is because being a part of such a gathering is the same as approving of that sin unless the individual has the intention of stopping them or transforming the gathering into one which is positive and where good is performed. This is actually a major responsibility in Islam and it is known as 'commanding the good and forbidding the evil'. When someone looks at something that is sinful while he is indifferent towards what is happening, it creates a spirit within them where the ugliness of that sin is lessened and the individual is slowly made accustomed to the performance of that sin.

[1] Uṣūl al-Kāfī, vol. 2, p. 374.

One Hundred and Twenty One
Engage in Works of Agriculture

Tradition:

ازْرَعُوا واغْرِسُوا وَاللهِ ما عَمِلَ النَّاسُ عَمَلًا أَحَلَّ وَلا أَطْيَبَ مِنْهُ

Imam Ṣādiq (ʿa) is narrated to have said: Engage in agriculture and the planting of trees for I swear by God that the people have not performed purer or more lawful (Ḥalāl) work than this.[1]

Brief Commentary:

Farming is one of the foundational aspects which human life is based upon and much of what people in society do would be impossible without it. Industrial factories and businesses would be unsustainable without established agriculture and farming, and this is because without the raw products provided by agriculture, factories and businessmen would not have the base products necessary for their work. Another interesting aspect of farming is that while it is possible to cheat and adulterate when it comes to other lines of work, such a thing is not possible when it comes to farming. At the end of the day, fruit is fruit and only so much can be done to it. Farmers must also work hard and their work is honest work; it is for this reason that this tradition has considered agriculture as being one of the most wholesome and pure lines of work that can be performed.

---

[1] Safīnat al-Biḥār, vol. 1, p. 549.

Lesson One Hundred and Twenty Two
The Duration of Life

Tradition:

مَوْتُ الإِنْسانِ بِالذُّنوبِ أَكْثَرُ مِنْ مَوْتِهِ بِالأَجَلِ وَحَياتُهُ بِالبِرِّ أَكْثَرُ مِنْ حَياتِهِ بِالعُمْرِ

Imam ʿAlī (ʿa) is narrated to have said: Death which arrives earlier for human beings as a result of sin is more common than death which comes as a result of one's natural lifespan; and the extended lifespan of people as a result of their good deeds is more common than their actual natural life spans.[1]

Brief Commentary:

Without any doubt, various sins are known to directly affect the length of our lives in a negative fashion. Such things as drinking alcohol, gambling, miserliness, and envy are known to have such an effect. In addition to these sins, there are other things which exert an indirect effect on one's lifespan. These indirect actors work through destabilizing the society, destroying public safety and security, and bringing about conflict and war. These indirect factors include things like usury and oppression.

At the same time, positive actions have their own deep effects on the calm and tranquility that people feel within their souls and their conscience, and this affects the length of their life spans in a positive manner. Therefore, we should realize that sins not only have spiritual effects, but they certainly have physical effects as well. These physical effects can go as far as affecting the quality of our physical lives, as well as how long we get to live.

---

[1] Safīnat al-Biḥār, p. 489.

Lesson One Hundred and Twenty Three
Cooperation with Satan

Tradition:

لا تَسُبَّنَّ إبْلِيسَ فِي العَلانِيَةِ وَأَنْتَ صَدِيقُهُ فِي السِّرِّ

Imam ʿAlī (ʿa) is narrated to have said: Do not curse Satan openly while you are his friend in secret.[1]

Brief Commentary:

Many people express a distaste and hatred for certain concepts like poverty, hypocrisy, Satan, and other such negative things. While they express such hatred outwardly, they are practically engulfed in the very same things they profess to hate. For example, there are some extremely wealthy individuals who fear poverty to such a degree that they live their lives just like the poverty stricken they so fear; they are terrified of spending any money and so they deprive themselves of everything in life. Similarly, there are some hypocrites who are busy constantly insulting and deprecating hypocrisy; yet they themselves are engulfed in hypocrisy from head to toe!

There are others who are greatly influenced by Satan and yet they constantly express negative words in regards to Satan. This is while they openly do what God has made unlawful and they easily allow themselves to be influenced and controlled by Satan himself. Therefore, the people should be aware that it is not enough to simply express an idea or concept outwardly; rather, they must internally manifest that concept as well.

---

[1] Turāth al-Aʿimmah, p. 209.

Lesson One Hundred and Twenty Four

Consult With Others so that You May Be Guided!

Tradition:

ما تَشاوَرَ قَوْمٌ إلّا هُدُوا إلى رُشْدِهِم

Imam Ḥasan ('a) is narrated to have said: No group consulted with one another in their works but that they were guided to their best interests.[1]

Brief Commentary:

When people cooperate and work together, this becomes a source of goodness and great blessings for them. They progress and are able to do things which would have been impossible for them individually. This is particularly true when it comes to intellectual and organizational issues, where the combined ideas of many have an especially powerful effect. Some people are unfortunately affected by a sense of stubbornness when it comes to the issue of consultation and so they refuse to seek the advice of others.

Such people find themselves constantly making mistakes and being entangled in various problems. The reason behind this is that each individual is able to see one facet of an issue (or at least only several facets). It is very rare to find someone who is able to look at an issue from all the possible angles. Therefore, when people consult others, they are able to more fully understand a given issue and this aids them in making a more comprehensive decision. Such decisions will almost always be stronger and more correct than a decision made by

[1] Tuḥaf al-'Uqūl, p. 164.

someone who can only see one side of the issue! Let us make a firm decision to always consult others during appropriate circumstances for this is the way to success and proper decision making in life.

Lesson One Hundred and Twenty Five
Salām is the Islamic Greeting

Tradition:

لِلسَّلامِ سَبْعُونَ حَسَنَةً تِسْعَةٌ وَسِتُّونَ لِلْمُبْتَدِئِ وَوَاحِدَةٌ لِلرَّادِ

Imam Ḥusayn ('a) is narrated to have said: The Salām has 70 rewards of which 69 of them are for the initiator of the greeting, while 1 of them is for the one who responds.[1]

Brief Commentary:

Amongst all the greetings that people around the world give to one another, the Islamic greeting has a particularly special nature and luminosity. This is because it is both a welcoming greeting, as well as a sign of peace, happiness, and friendship. At the same time, it also conveys well wishes for the person's health and soundness (physical, mental, and spiritual). It is for this same reason that the greeting of the dwellers of paradise is the Salām; the angels also greet the people who have lived pure lives with this greeting.

Unfortunately, some amongst the Muslims believes that initiating the greeting or replying is actually a sign of weakness. They therefore abstain from greeting others or from replying to their greeting. What they don't understand is that by not greeting others, they are missing out on a great virtue, and the aforementioned tradition has explained how great the rewards are for such an action.

---

[1] Tuḥaf al-'Uqūl, p. 177.

LESSON ONE HUNDRED AND TWENTY SIX
THE SEPARATION OF BELIEF AND ACTION!

Tradition:

أَلا وَأَنَّ أَبْغَضَ النَّاسِ إِلى اللهِ مَنْ يَقْتَدِي بِسُنَّةِ إِمامٍ وَلا يَقْتَدِي بِأَعْمالِهِ

Imam Zayn al-ʿAbidīn is narrated to have said: The most detested of the people in front of God is he who has accepted an Imam and a leader, but does not follow him in regards to his actions.[1]

Brief Commentary:

One of the biggest defiencies that people commonly face is the separation between what they believe and what they actually do in their lives. Some people may speak about how much they like or believe in something, but when you look at their actions, you see that they are effectively not living based on those professed beliefs.

Such people may believe in God for example, but their actions may practically show them as being someone who doesn't believe in God. Another individual may believe in God's justice on the Day of Judgement, but when you look at their morals and ethics, you see that such a person is practically a disbeliever when it comes to the Day of Judgement.

Such an individual may consider the Prophet of Islam (ṣ) as the greatest of the prophets, and Imam ʿAlī (ʿa) as the greatest of leaders, and yet his actions will not at all be in concordance with theirs. In light of this tradition, we should always be careful that our beliefs and our actions are in line with one another, for such is the mark of the real believer.

---

[1] Tuḥaf al-ʿUqūl, p. 202.

Lesson One Hundred and Twenty Seven
God's Punishment

Tradition:

إنَّ للَّهِ عُقُوباتٌ فِي القُلُوبِ وَالأَبْدانِ:

ضَنَكٌ فِي المَعِيشَةِ وَوَهْنٌ فِي العِبادَةِ وَما ضُرِبَ عَبْدٌ بِعُقُوبَةٍ أَعْظَمُ مِنْ قَسْوَةِ القَلْبِ

Imam Bāqir (ʻa) is narrated to have said: God has punishments which affect the body and the soul. (These include): reduced sustenance and feebleness in worship, but God has not punished any of his servants with a more severe punishment than that of hard heartedness.[1]

Brief Commentary:

Divine punishments are in reality the natural reactions that people earn in place of their negative actions. In some cases, these punishments come in the form of an unbalanced income flow, while in other cases, they come in the form of a lack of vitality in worship and one's connection to God. Yet, the most important and dangerous form of punishment comes in the form of a hardness of heart. This is when one's heart becomes empty of human emotion and feeling, and where it becomes devoid of all feelings of friendship and social connection. Such a condition is the root of a great many sins and evil actions.

[1] Tuḥaf al-ʻUqūl, p. 217.

Lesson One Hundred and Twenty Eight
A Reality Has Been Forgotten

Tradition:

لَمْ يَخْلُقِ اللهُ يَقِينًا لَاشَكَّ فِيْهِ أَشْبَهَ بِشَكٍّ لا يَقِينَ فِيْهِ مِنَ المَوتِ

Imam Ṣādiq (ʻa) is narrated to have said: God has not created any certainty like death while it is as if it were a doubt in which there was never any certainty.[1]

Brief Commentary:

This is a beautiful statement which mentions how unaware people are of the issue of death in spite of its certain nature. If people have doubts in anything in their lives, the one thing which is 100% certain is that our lives will end and everyone will leave this world. This is a certainty even for those who don't believe in any afterlife or religion. In spite of this, people live their lives in a way as if such a thing does not exist and they will live forever.

Since people live their lives in this way, they don't prepare themselves for what is eventually to come; they fail to perform good deeds and acts of worship. They don't attempt to purify their souls and strengthen their faith. We should always keep death in clear view, and strive to purify our souls in order that when the end does arrive, we don't leave this world ashamed and embarrassed of what we have failed to accomplish and become.

[1] Tuḥaf al-ʻUqūl, p. 271.

Lesson One Hundred and Twenty Nine
The Position of Knowledge and Wisdom

Tradition:

إنَّ الزَّرْعَ يَنْبُتُ فِي السَّهْلِ وَلا يَنْبُتُ فِي الصَّفا فَكَذلك الحِكْمَةُ تَعْمُرُ فِي قَلْبِ المُتَواضِعِ وَلا تَعْمُرُ فِي قَلْبِ المُتَكَبِّرِ الجَبارِ

Imam Kāẓim ('a) is narrated to have said: Plants grow on soft soil and not on stones. Similarly, knowledge and wisdom sprout only in a humble heart and not in a heart that is filled with arrogance.[1]

Brief Commentary:

The first step in gaining knowledge is the possession of humility. One must have humility in the face of the truth, in the face of one's teacher, and in the face of everyone who knows more and is able to teach us something. Due to this reason, ignorance and arrogance are usually two attributes that come together.

The arrogant are never ready to acknowledge their lack of knowledge and their ignorance. In some cases, they may even deny something that is true when it doesn't correspond with their beliefs or actions. In some cases, this denial will even extend into open resistance! In addition, the arrogant are never willing to hear the truth from anyone they consider to be of a lower rank than themselves and so they remain submerged in a state of compound ignorance throughout their lives.

---

[1] Tuḥaf al-'Uqūl, p. 296.

LESSON ONE HUNDRED AND THIRTY
THE HEAVY DUTIES OF THE IMAM ('A)

Tradition:

الإِمَامُ أَمِينُ اللهِ فِي أَرْضِهِ وَخَلْقِهِ وَحُجَّتُهُ عَلَى عِبَادِهِ وَخَلِيفَتُهُ فِي بِلاَدِهِ
وَالدَّاعِي إِلَى اللهِ وَالذَّابُّ عَنْ حَرِيمِ اللهِ

Imam Riḍā ('a) is narrated to have said: The Imam is the
trustworthy of God on this earth and amongst God's creation.
He is his proof amongst his servants and his deputy in the cities. He is the one who invites (the people) towards God and he
is the defender of God's sanctum.[1]

Brief Commentary:

This tradition is just a section of the longer whole which
introduces the position of the Imamate. It describes five of the
important and heavy responsibilities which the Imam ('a) has:

1- The Imam is the protector of the divine revelation; he
protects all of the knowledge of the religion.

2- The Imam is the living proof of God's religion.

3- The Imam is the guardian of the divine and he is his
representative amongst the people.

4- The Imam is the propagator of the religion and he is
the one who commands towards the good and forbids
against the evil.

5- The Imam is the defender of the divine sanctuary
against the encroachment of the enemy. Such a person
must possess divine knowledge and the rank of infalli-
bility; no one except God can select an individual for
such a position.

---

[1] Tuḥaf al-'Uqūl, p. 328.

Lesson One Hundred and Thirty One
The Closed Doors Will Be Opened!

Tradition:

لَو كَانَتِ السَّماواتُ وَالأَرضُ رَتْقًا عَلى عَبْدٍ ثُمَّ اتَّقى الله تعالى لَجَعَلَ الله لَهُ مِنْها مَخْرَجًا

Imam Jawād (ʻa) is narrated to have said: If the doors of the heavens and the earth are closed for someone but he begins to implement and practice piety, then God will make easy his work.[1]

Brief Commentary:

Sometimes in life, it appears that all the doors have been closed to us and everywhere that we look, we are faced with difficulties and problems. Such circumstances are an opportunity for us to wake up and return back to God. Such a return will be one that is constructive and transformative; when we connect to God through such means and ask help from him, God will aid us and send his mercy upon us. Doors will begin to open which we never even imagined existed. In reality, these situations are a great opportunity, even though they initially may have seemed like a calamity instead.

---

[1] Nūr al-Abṣār, p. 150.

Lesson One Hundred and Thirty Two
Be Careful of People with No Character

Tradition:

مَنْ هانَتْ عَلَيهِ نَفْسُهُ فَلا تَأْمَنْ شَرَّهُ

Imam Hādī (ʿa) is narrated to have said: Be careful of the evil of those who have no character![1]

Brief Commentary:

One of the most important things which prevents evil actions and corruption is that of character and self respect, or at the very least, a sense of character and self respect. Those individuals who have character, even if they are looked down upon by others, will always maintain a standard of good behavior because of the self respect which they have for themselves. Yet, if these same people felt that they had no character or that the people had no respect for them, then they might perform all kinds of evil actions. This is why the Imam (ʿa) is saying that we should be careful of such people.

It is for this same reason that one of the important facets of training and educating one's children is through the creation of self respect and character for them. When a child senses that he is worthy and the people respect him, this will result in him being careful of what he does both publicly and privately, and so this prevents him from a great many sins and evil actions.

---

[1] Tuḥaf al-ʿUqūl, p. 362.

Lesson One Hundred and Thirty Three
The Greater Jihād

Tradition:

أَشَدُّ النَّاسِ اجْتِهادًا مَنْ تَرَكَ الذُّنوبَ

Imam Ḥasan 'Askarī ('a) is narrated to have said: The strongest warrior is he who stops sinning.[1]

Brief Commentary:

In Islam, the battle against our negative desires and lusts (which are the main root of various sins) is called the Greater Jihād. Such a fight is considered to be more important than the fight against one's enemies. This is because such a fight is the means to self purification, and until self purification has taken place, victory over one's enemies is also not possible. This is because defeat against one's enemies is usually the result of personal weakness due to this lack of character and self purification.

The value of this battle is much greater in a society that is filled with corruption and it will yield much clearer results. The victory of the Prophet (ṣ) in the city of Medina was a direct result of the internal battles and character building that took place for the companions while they were in the city of Mecca.

---

[1] Biḥār al-Anwār, vol. 78, p. 383.

Lesson One Hundred and Thirty Four
During the Occultation of the Mahdī (ʿa)

Tradition:

أمّا الحَوادِثُ الوَاقِعَةُ فَارْجِعُوا فِيها إلى رُواةِ أحادِيثِنا

Imam Mahdī (ʿa) is narrated to have said: Refer to the narrators of our traditions during the various events that will take place during the time of the Greater Occultation.[1]

Brief Commentary:

Society cannot be properly organized and its member's full potential realized without proper leadership. For this reason, God has never left his servants to themselves without any form of divine leadership and guidance. There have always been divine leaders amongst us who have helped to guide us towards the way that is best.

Even during the time of the occultation of Imam Mahdī (ʿa), there were select deputies, as well as general deputies who would guide the people through him. These were men of faith and knowledge who were and are well acquainted with the Quran and the Sunnah of the Ahl al-Bayt. These are the necessary qualifications for such a position and anyone else who claims this position is not qualified at all.

[1] A section of the famous letter from the Imam (ʿa) as taken from various sources.

Lesson One Hundred and Thirty Five
The Root of All Evils

Tradition:

اجْتَنِبُوا الخَمْرَ فَإِنَّها مِفْتَاحُ كُلِّ شَرٍّ

The Prophet (ṣ) is narrated to have said: Stay away from wine (alcohol) for it is the key to all evils.[1]

Brief Commentary:

Many books and articles have been written on the ill effects of alcohol, and its negative effects have been proven on the nervous system, the heart, the blood vessels, the digestive system, the liver, the kidneys, and practically all of the organs of the body. Besides these physically based negative effects, alcohol is related to a great many social ills as well. The statistics on the social dangers of alcohol are truly astounding. These words of the Prophet (ṣ) are enough for us to understand that alcohol is key to many of the evils of this world.

[1] Nahj al-Faṣāḥah, p. 1.

Lesson One Hundred and Thirty Six
Performing One's Duty is the Greatest Worship

Tradition:

مَنْ عَمِلَ بِما افْتَرَضَ الله عَلَيْهِ فَهُوَ مِنْ أَعْبَدِ النّاسِ

Imam Sajjād ('a) is narrated to have said: Whoever performs his necessary duties is the most worshipful of the people.[1]

Brief Commentary:

Worship is neither limited to serving God's creation, nor is it limited to only prayers and fasting. Rather, the greatest worship of God is that in which each person performs their own necessary duties. What kind of worship can be higher and greater than the one through which a society can be transformed into a virtual utopia filled with all sorts of blessings and goodness.

What is important to note is that performing one's duties is a term of wide ranging meaning and it also includes doing one's duty in terms of the obligatory worship as well. So in reality doing one's duty includes all of the necessary social, cultural, and economic actions possible. This is in direct contradiction to those who believe that religiosity is found in putting aside all worldly duties and simply engaging in acts of ritual worship.

---

[1] Wasā'il al-Shī'ah, vol. 11, p. 206.

Lesson One Hundred and Thirty Seven
The Inhabitants of the Stars

Tradition:

هٰذه النُّجُومُ الّتي فِي السَّماء مَدَائِنٌ مِثْلَ المَدَائِنِ الّتي فِي الأَرْضِ مَرْبُوطَةٌ كُلُّ مَدينَةٍ إلى عَمُودٍ مِنْ نُورٍ

Imam ʿAlī (ʿa) is narrated to have said: These stars which are in the skies have cities much like the cities of the earth; each of their cities are connected with a column of light with other cities.[1]

Brief Commentary:

It is extremely selfish of us to imagine that all of the planets and all of the stars in the universe are completely void and empty of inhabitants. The scientists of today have done certain calculations where they have figured that there should be at least millions, if not hundreds of millions of planets which contain inhabitants in the universe. There is a strong possibility that many of these planets have their own advanced civilizations, some of which may be even more advanced than that which is found on this earth. The reason behind this advanced state is due to the fact that life on those planets began many thousands or even millions of years before that of earth. The tradition above is one of the scientific miracles of Imam ʿAlī (ʿa), which was mentioned over fourteen centuries ago.

---

[1] Safīnat al-Biḥār, vol. 3, p. 574.

Lesson One Hundred and Thirty Eight
The Quran and the Law of Gravity

Tradition:

أَلَيْسَ الله يَقُولُ: «بِغَيرِ عَمَدٍ تَرَوْنَها»؟

فَقُلْتُ: بَلى

قَالَ: ثُمَّ عَمَدٍ، وَلَكِن، لا تَرَوْنَها

Imam Riḍā ('a) is narrated to have said to one of his friends: Does not God say that the skies are established without any pillar (support structure) that can be seen? His friend replied: Indeed. The Imam ('a) then said: Therefore, there exists a pillar which is invisible and you are not able to see it.[1]

Brief Commentary:

Today, it is firmly established that the earth and all of the planets travel in their set orbits through the balance given to them by the phenomenon of gravity. The laws of attraction act much like a great chain which pulls things together, while the law of repellence pushes things away from each other. This perfect balance has allowed all of these immense planets to travel along their own orbits without the least bit of deviation. This is that same invisible pillar which the Quran has mentioned. What is amazing is that these words were spoken over 1400 years ago at a time when the people were completely unaware of such matters; this is a great proof of the truthfulness of this religion and its message.

[1] Tafsīr Burhān, vol. 3, p. 278.

Lesson One Hundred and Thirty Nine
The Secret of the Mountains!

Tradition:

وَوَتَّدَ بِالصُّخُورِ مَيدانَ أَرْضِهِ

Imam 'Alī ('a) is narrated to have said: Through means of the mountains, the earth is prevented from shaking and moving.[1]

Brief Commentary:

Today it has been proven that the moon exerts an influence on the tides and causes their rise and fall each day and night. Due to the effect of the pull of the moon, water levels in the ocean can rise one meter, and in some cases, even up to fifteen meters in height. In the same way that the moon's pull affects the tides, it also affects the earth's crust as well. The crust is pulled up at least thirty centimeters, after which it contracts again back to its normal condition.

What keeps the earth's surface stable and firm is the existence of the mountains whose roots are connected to one another and which form a network all around the earth. The presence of these mountains prevents the earth's crust from shaking and causes it be stable and firm. If the mountains did not exist and the earth continuously was expanding and contracting, then how would the people be able to live? This is a reality which the Imams ('a) mentioned over 1400 years ago.

---

[1] Nahj al-Balāghah, sermon 1.

Lesson One Hundred and Forty

Microscopic Creatures

Tradition:

إنَّما قُلْنا «اللَّطِيفُ» لِلْخَلْقِ اللَّطِيفِ ... وَما لا تَكَادُ عُيُونُنا تَسْتَبِيْنُهُ لِدِمامَةِ خَلْقِها، لا تَراهُ عُيُونُنا وَلا تَلْمُسُهُ أَيدِينا

Imam Riḍā ('a) is narrated to have said: The reason God is called the Subtle (Al-Laṭīf) is because of his creation of very small and delicate creatures... These are creatures that we can't see and our hands can't feel due to their extremely small size.[1]

Brief Commentary:

This is just a small section of a larger tradition which Fatḥ ibn Yazdād Jurjānī has narrated from Imam Riḍā ('a). In this tradition, it has been explained that these creatures are so small that our senses cannot perceive them at all. They live amongst the waves of the ocean, the layers of the bark of the trees, as well as scattered amongst the deserts and plains. This tradition has been narrated in books that are more than a thousand years old. They were compiled hundreds of years before the birth of Pasteur. This is a clear cut scientific miracle that has been narrated from Imam Riḍā ('a).

---

[1] Kitāb Wāfī, vol. 1, p. 106.

Lesson One Hundred and Forty One

They Just Carry The Name of Muslims!

Tradition:

يَأتِي عَلَى النَّاسِ زَمانٌ لا يَبْقَى فِيهِمْ مِنَ القُرآنِ إلّا رَسْمُهُ وَمِنَ الإسلامِ إلّا اسْمُهُ، مَساجِدُهُمْ يَوْمَئِذٍ عامِرَةٌ مِنَ البِناءِ، خَرابٌ مِنَ الهُدى

Imam ʻAlī (ʻa) is narrated to have said: A time will come for the people when only lines will remain of the Quran, and only a name will remain of Islam, and the mosques of the Muslims will be beautiful in construction but empty of guidance and salvation![1]

Brief Commentary:

It cannot be said if this prediction has been fulfilled or if it relates to a future era but what is certain is that some aspects of it are apparent today within our society. What is stranger yet is that such Muslims are always complaining of a lack of progress and it is as if they think that only the name of Islam and the written lines of the Quran are enough as a religion. They don't see the Quran as a book of education and human progress, nor do they see Islam as a complete way of life that includes intellectual and scientific development.

[1] Aphorisms, Number 369.

Lesson One Hundred and Forty Two

The Measure of the Intellect and Ignorance

Tradition:

اللِّسَانُ مِعيارٌ إطاشَةِ الجَهْلِ وَارْجَحِةِ العَقْلِ

Imam 'Alī ('a) is narrated to have said: The tongue is the measure of the overflowing of ignorance and the measure of the intellect and wisdom.[1]

Brief Commentary:

The most important gateway into the soul of man and his character can be found in his tongue. It is the tongue that is the means to best measuring someone's intellect. With just a small movement, the tongue is capable of revealing the deepest motivations and intentions which someone can hide behind. It is for this same reason that many of the commandments of Islam revolve around the reformation of the tongue and the Infallibles ('a) have repeatedly warned of the dangers that can be found in the tongue. It is also obvious that the tongue cannot be reformed unless the spirit and the thoughts of an individual are first reformed. At the same time, it is possible through much silence and care to prevent many of the dangers that can arise from the tongue.

---

[1] Tuḥaf al-'Uqūl, p. 143.

Lesson One Hundred and Forty Three Something Greater Than a Blessing!

Tradition:

الشَّاكِرُ أَسْعَدُ بِالشُّكْرِ مِنْهُ بِالنِّعْمَةِ الّتي أَوجَبَتْ الشُّكْرَ لأَنّ النِّعَمَ مَتاعٌ وَالشُّكْرَ نِعَمٌ وَعُقْبى

Imam Hādī (ʻa) is narrated to have said: The felicity of expressing thanks for a blessing is greater than one's felicity for having received that blessing. This is because blessings are a means for the life of this world and thankfulness is an investment both for this world and the next.[1]

Brief Commentary:

Thankfulness is not limited to simply expressing words through one's tongue; it also includes one's actions as well. Being truly thankful includes utilizing the blessings that one has received in the proper way. Being thankful in such a way brings about even further blessings which may make the initial blessing seem small and insignificant. When blessings are utilized in the way of God and the happiness of his creation, it becomes a further investment for the felicity of both this world and the next. This is while if we look at a blessing itself, it may simply be a material blessing, while thankfulness for it extends much higher and is of greater value!

---

[1] Tuḥaf al-ʻUqūl, p. 362.

Lesson One Hundred and Forty Four

Invigorating the School of Thought of the Ahl al-Bayt

Tradition:

مَنْ جَلَسَ مَجْلِسًا يُحيي فِيْهِ أَمْرَنا لَمْ يَمُتْ قَلْبُهُ يَومَ تَمُوتُ القُلُوبُ

Imam Riḍā ('a) is narrated to have said: The heart of anyone who sits in a gathering which invigorates our school of thought will not die on the day when hearts die![1]

Brief Commentary:

It is apparent from this tradition that one of the certain duties of the followers of the Ahl al-Bayt is to constantly enliven their ideology. This includes helping people to understand this school of thought, gain access to its teachings, and taste the essence of the words of the Imams ('a). These should be gatherings of preparation, self building, and spirituality, and not gatherings of simple amusement or those in which people simply seek out their material wants and desires, while forgetting their social and spiritual problems. These are gatherings in which the hearts are awakened and given life once again.

[1] Mīrāth Imāmān, p. 443.

Lesson One Hundred and Forty Five
Safeguarding The Secrets

Tradition:

إِذا حَدَّثَ الرَّجُلُ بِحَدِيثٍ، ثُمَّ الْتَفَتَ فَهِيَ أَمانَةٌ

The Prophet (ṣ) is narrated to have said: When someone says something and then looks around, his words are a secret and a trust (and one must strive to preserve them).[1]

Brief Commentary:

A trust has many various forms in Islam and one of these forms is through preserving the secrets of the people. This is considered to be so important in Islam that revealing the secrets of the people is counted as one of the greater sins. It isn't even necessary for an individual to mention that what he is telling you should be kept a secret; it is enough for him to simply look around in a certain manner and be careful of those who are within range. This is enough for such words to be considered a secret and to make their safeguarding obligatory.

[1] Nahj al-Faṣāḥah, p. 38.

Lesson One Hundred and Forty Six
The Signs of Faith!

Tradition:

إذا سَرَّتْكَ حَسَنَتُكَ وَساءَتْكَ سَيِّئَتُكَ فَأَنْتَ مُؤمِنٌ

The Prophet (ṣ) is narrated to have said: At the time that your good actions make you happy and your bad actions make you sad, then you are a believing individual.[1]

Brief Commentary:

Islam has mentioned that everyone is born with a pure inner nature; this includes an intrinsic faith in God and a love of all that is good. As time passes, it is possible for sins to gradually affect the soul and influence it in such a way where it is completely transformed from this original state. In spite of this, as long as someone loves what is good and hates what is bad, it is clear that the spirit of faith and their pure inner nature is still present and healthy within them. It is truly the wretched who don't become sad at their evil actions and a step beyond this is when they actually become happy!

---

[1] Nahj al-Faṣāḥah, p. 41.

Lesson One Hundred and Forty Seven
The First Condition of Every Action

Tradition:

ما مِنْ حَرَكَةٍ إلّا وَأَنْتَ مُحْتاجٌ فِيْها إلى مَعْرِفَةٍ

Imam 'Alī ('a) is narrated to have said: There is no action or work except that you need awareness, comprehension, and understanding in its performance.[1]

Brief Commentary:

If we reflect on the words of 'There is no action or work…' we will become familiar with the extent of the Islamic program for life. The religion of Islam isn't only a program for worship and supplication, or only a belief without any practical applications. Islam is in reality a program for the entirety of our lives and this includes both personal issues, as well as social issues. This program extends for every action that we perform. The first step towards enacting this program is awareness and understanding of the reality; without understanding ourselves and the reality properly, all of our actions and efforts will be without effect or at least they will be lessened in their effectiveness.

---

[1] Safīnat al-Biḥār, vol. 1, p. 15.

Lesson One Hundred and Forty Eight
The Importance of Guests

Tradition:

إِذا أَرَادَ اللهُ بِقَومٍ خَيْراً أَهدَى إِلَيْهِمْ هَدِيَةً قَالُوا: وَما تِلكَ الهَدِيَةُ؟ قَالَ: الضَّيْفُ

The Prophet (ṣ) is narrated to have said: Whenever God wishes goodness and felicity for someone, he gives them a gift. He was asked what gift does he give? He replied: Guests![1]

Brief Commentary:

Without any doubt, guests are a great gift from the divine who possess value and honor. Unfortunately, in today's materialistically oriented world, human emotions have been seemingly downgraded or even completely destroyed. Due to this reason, having guests has lost much of its meaning in many parts of the world today. In some cases, they are even seen as an annoyance and a bother, and it is becoming rarer for people to invite others to their home or to accept invitations unless there is a type of economic or political (materialistically oriented) motivation involved. Yet if we look at much of the Muslim world or within specific religious families, we will see that guests are greatly honored even if they are not well known to the host family. We should always keep in mind that guests are a gift from God and we should treat and honor them accordingly.

---

[1] Biḥār al-Anwār, vol. 15, p. 241.

LESSON ONE HUNDRED AND FORTY NINE
RESPECT AND LOVE

Tradition:

لَيْسَ مِنَّا مَن لَمْ يُوقِّرْ كَبِيرَنا وَلَمْ يَرْحَمْ صَغِيرَنا

Imam Ṣādiq ('a) is narrated to have said: He who does not respect the elders and is not affectionate towards the young is not from us![1]

Brief Commentary:

Human society is much like a caravan that is always in motion; children are born and soon grow up while the adults age and become older, eventually passing away. No one amongst these travelers can bypass this process. In this caravan, the elders usually have more experience and wisdom due to the lives that they've lived. If they've lived their lives properly, they are also the source of much good in this world. Due to this reason, they are to be respected and honored by those who are younger than them. At the same time, the youth are newer to this world and they are just starting their lives; due to this reason, they must be loved and treated with complete care and consideration. This is the proper way that the youth and the elders are to be treated in a balanced and caring society.

---

[1] Uṣūl al-Kāfī, vol. 3, p. 253.

Lesson One Hundred and Fifty

Invest For Yourself In This Way!

Tradition:

ما تُقَدِّمُ مِنْ خَيْرٍ يَبْقَ لَكَ ذُخْرُهُ وَما تُؤَخِّرُهُ يَكُنْ لِغَيْرِكَ خَيْرُهُ

Imam 'Alī ('a) is narrated to have said: What you send ahead of yourselves will be saved for you and what you delay will end up benefitting others (while its responsibility will remain yours).[1]

Brief Commentary:

It appears that the desire of people to accumulate wealth has increased during modern times to much higher levels than before. Unfortunately, such people accumulate wealth without considering what their main goal in life is and at some point, it really does seem like an illogical and even insane thing to do. Such people get so involved in the accumulation of wealth that they sometimes lose sight of whether they are making that money through lawful or unlawful means. In addition, have such people thought about the fact that they will not be able to take their wealth with them when they leave this world, nor will they be able to spend all of it within their lives. At some point, they will have to leave all of their wealth and the only thing that will remain with them will be the responsibility of the wealth that they have left behind.

[1] Nahj al-Balāghah.

Notes

www.ingramcontent.com/pod-product-compliance
Lightning Source LLC
Chambersburg PA
CBHW031524120626
46545CB00005B/1993
* 9 7 8 1 9 5 6 2 7 6 3 7 4 *